I Don't Hate the South

I Don't Hate the South

REFLECTIONS ON FAULKNER, FAMILY, AND THE SOUTH

HOUSTON A. BAKER, JR.

OXFORD
UNIVERSITY PRESS
2007

OXFORD
UNIVERSITY PRESS

Oxford University Press, Inc., publishes works that further
Oxford University's objective of excellence
in research, scholarship, and education.

Oxford   New York
Auckland   Cape Town   Dar es Salaam   Hong Kong   Karachi
Kuala Lumpur   Madrid   Melbourne   Mexico City   Nairobi
New Delhi   Shanghai   Taipei   Toronto

With offices in
Argentina   Austria   Brazil   Chile   Czech Republic   France   Greece
Guatemala   Hungary   Italy   Japan   Poland   Portugal   Singapore
South Korea   Switzerland   Thailand   Turkey   Ukraine   Vietnam

Copyright © 2007 by Oxford University Press, Inc.

Published by Oxford University Press, Inc.
198 Madison Avenue, New York, New York 10016

www.oup.com

Oxford is a registered trademark of Oxford University Press

Library of Congress Cataloging-in-Publication Data
Baker, Houston A.
I don't hate the South : reflections on Faulkner, family, and the South /
Houston A. Baker, Jr.
    p. cm.
Includes bibliographical references.
ISBN 978-0-19-508429-0; 978-0-19-532655-0 (pbk.)
1. American literature—Southern States—History and criticism.
2. Faulkner, William, 1897–1962—Criticism and interpretation. 3. American literature—
African American authors—History and criticism. 4. Southern States—
In literature. 5. Southern States—Race relations. 6. Racism—Southern States.
7. Baker, Houston A. 8. African American College teachers—Biography.
9. African American families—Southern States—Biography. I. Title.
PS261.B24 2007
810.9'975—dc22   2006032637

9 8 7 6 5 4 3 2 1

Printed in the United States of America
on acid-free paper

THIS WORK IS DEDICATED with gratitude and appreciation to all who have stood by and shared friendship, wisdom, and love. I send magnums of gratitude to my wife, Charlotte. I am grateful as well to our son, Mark, and his wife, Michelle, and their family. My in-laws are extraordinary, especially my nephews, Ben and Greg. All of them have "lifted me up on eagles' wings." My extended writing family includes the generous and forbearing agent Jane Dystel, without whom nothing is possible. The same is true of my assistant, Lincoln Hancock, who not only turned his editorial eye on all pages of this book, but also processed the pages in completely reliable and efficient fashion. Naming friends must always be undertaken with circumspection. However, I have no reservations where the present project is concerned when I thank Isabel, Ana, Heather, Lauren, Priscilla, Arnold, Cathy, and Frances. I take sole responsibility for all mistakes. I do so because I know I can call on family for steadfastness and love when such mistakes are discovered, alleged, or denounced. This realization of who, beyond question, is "for you" is surely a southern family habit of mind.

Pastoral

In the dream, I am with the Fugitive
Poets. We're gathered for a photograph.
Behind us, the skyline of Atlanta
hidden by the photographer's backdrop—
a lush pasture, green, full of soft-eyed cows
lowing, a chant that sounds like *no, no. Yes,*
I say to the glass of bourbon I'm offered.
We're lining up now—Robert Penn Warren,
his voice just audible above the drone
of bulldozers, telling us where to stand.
Say "race," the photographer croons. I'm in
blackface again when the flash freezes us.
My father's white, I tell them, *and rural.*
You don't hate the South, they ask. *You don't hate it?*

—Natasha Trethewey, *Native Guard: Poems* (2006)

SHREVELIN MCCANNON: "Now I want you to tell me just one more thing. Why do you hate the South?"

QUENTIN COMPSON: "I dont hate it," Quentin said, quickly, at once, immediately; "I dont hate it," he said. *I dont hate it* he thought, panting in the cold air, the iron New England dark: *I dont. I don't. I dont hate it! I dont hate it.*

—William Faulkner, *Absalom, Absalom!*

Contents

Introduction

I have worried the lines of "race" and "place" for more than a few years. So when I was invited to deliver a lecture at the 2002 Faulkner & Yoknapatawpha Conference at the University of Mississippi, I had an immediate sense of intellectual satisfaction. In fact, I had wanted to participate in the conference from the moment I saw the announcement of its inaugural meeting in Oxford twenty-nine years ago. I was teaching at the University of Virginia in Charlottesville then. I was not a Faulkner scholar; I was not a professor of southern literature. I was not even an Americanist, in any formal sense of the term. Yet my early and intuitive understanding of Afro-American literature and culture led me to believe—quite naively, I am now aware—that I had something useful to say at that first conference. For at the time, I had begun to know the critical importance of my own southern origins with respect to my own peculiar understanding of life.

Of course, as a literary critic trained in the American higher educational project of my day (roughly, the 1960s), I had learned that in the worlds of literature and culture William Faulkner and "the

South" were virtually synonymous. Speak one, and you naturally implied the other: Faulkner/the South, united. Hence, I felt that by bringing to bear my newly formed wisdom about black literature, culture, and the South in clever and regional ways, I would be able to enlighten the conference—as well as travel safely into the deeper American South under a semi-protective banner of academia, garnering what I imagined would be invaluable and inspiriting influences from the homeland of the Bard of Rowan Oaks.

It didn't work out. Egotistical fantasy had gotten the better of me. There was no reason for the conference organizers even to know my name, much less invite me to the conference.

So, after twenty-nine years, I finally got my invitation to Oxford, Mississippi—my pass to southern travel and articulation. I accepted with enthusiasm, and submitted the tentative title "Traveling with Faulkner" for my keynote. "This," I thought, "has been a long time coming." I hoped to construct an autobiographical account of my dealings with Faulkner, to learn more about him as I went along, and to do a stellar job at the conference. It all seemed a happy prospect in the fall of 2001.

But then came the spring and summer of 2002, in which I commenced to think about what I *really* had to say about Faulkner and, well, me. At first, the pickings seemed exceedingly slim—an old bone and a ragged chestnut or two from my literary critical past. That was it. So as that ultimate resort of we who read for a living, I bought the bulk of Faulkner's oeuvre in bright new paperback editions and set them on a shelf in my study, waiting for the books to speak. When all else fails, read.

By then, the summer heat in Durham, North Carolina—my new home and place of employment at Duke University—had turned into a blistering, record-breaking drought. Reservoirs sank to historic lows, and miserable black crows picked at the dry expanses of once-green lawns. It was a very good time to be indoors, air-conditioned, and reading an author in whose work the avaricious protagonists, dry as dust, are tragically incapable of providing water to anyone who thirsts—whether from estate cisterns or from more ethereal fountains of the spirit. During this hot, dry season in Durham I did not so much *read* Faulkner as journey into him and his work, traveling with the southern sage into the phantasmagoric world of Yoknapatawpha. I was preparing for Oxford, Mississippi—that site of American racial dread and horror. An uneasy anticipation of the trip and the conference gave me night sweats and a worrisome bundle of nerves.

My wife grew concerned as I began to show up for morning coffee with yet another new Faulkner paperback in hand. "When," she asked with loving solicitude, "do you think you will finish reading and actually *write* your talk?" "I don't know," I replied. "He is an extremely prolix author, and his cast of characters is confusing and gargantuan." My wife responded: "You mean you haven't found a thread to follow through the labyrinth, right?" She knows precisely when to call me out. For in truth I had no idea what shape my already titled keynote would assume. I was reading in desperate avoidance of trying to write.

But eventually, I did begin writing. The essay on Faulkner in the present family album reveals the shape of that labor. But the evolution of the essay, beginning at the keys of my computer during that long summer, is nearly impossible to describe. It was as though the southern bard—in all his dipsomaniac and mentally grievous genius and challenge—had taken hold of my consciousness and forced me to pay deep, abiding, nearly obsessive attention to matters of the South, race, and the routes taken and circumnavigated by transatlantic explorers of the Americas. He compelled me to smell the sweat of the combat of owners and the owned; to see the whole construction of a "region" as always nationally complex, always the fulcrum of what was required and in need of writing in order to save or damn the "American" enterprise. That summer was a global moment into which I had been solicited by my own desire and by the haunting prose of Faulkner's fiction. His words were a sonorous undertow pulling me into the monitory ethics of my father and his South. It was all very bizarre.

My writing that summer became a journey I shared with my son, who, after I read him a section of the essay, said: "Dad, you know that's like a fantastic voice speaking. And it isn't just your voice. It is not just you speaking. It's uncanny." I took this to be a positive evaluation.

I read another section to my wife. She said: "You cannot leave the South, or maybe even this house, because clearly your muse is here. You've never written anything like this before." My family speaks this way; they are literary and cultural studies buffs who believe in the spirit. Buoyed by their genuine astonishment, I soldiered on. And as I was completing the very last portion of the Faulkner talk, I sat watching, feeling, experiencing massive thunderclouds forming outside, trees commencing their dance, birds and squirrels scampering to shelter. The whole southern earth cavorted with a magical rhythm of foreknowledge. A storm approached. As I wrote the final two pages of the essay, clouds broke and rain poured, lightning struck, and the ground hissed steam from an immense, cool downpour. I found myself crying, I suppose, for the loss and gain of it all: the lessons of Faulkner, and the American geographies of race, region, family, and critical reparations that cannot be won without travel, or comprehended in the absence of some clear notion about our shared, complicated, harrowing, and heroic relationships in difference.

In the office of completed narratives, I can say my Faulkner keynote played extremely well in Mississippi. "I have been coming to this conference for twenty-nine years," said one elderly, clear-eyed white woman at the conclusion of my presentation. "And yours was the best talk I have ever heard!" Not all were as charitable, of course, but that woman's words were lovely recompense in Oxford, where the summer humidity was as thick as white crowds at a turn-of-the-century spectacle lynching.

Out of my experience with Faulkner grew the idea for a sort of black, southern family album of regional reflections. My recent work dealt with understanding the contours of race and institution formation, race and expressive cultural forms, race and region, under the banner of the American South. Why not bring all these matters into a single aggregation? For to travel in the regions of Afro-American literature, expressive culture, and intellectual musings; family and kinship relations; and scholarly endeavors designed pragmatically to shift white supremacy into other shapes is to travel American and global spaces and places of that great signifier, race. It is to discover startling connections: personal, familial, and scholarly.

It is to sample late-night fare in a Portuguese café, realizing the stone walkway on which you arrived may consist of ballast stones from slave ships that carried your African ancestors into horror. It is to turn a skeptical (somewhat fantastical, in fact) gaze on "Negroes" who have damned their black, southern ancestral "family" as ignorant or misguided provincials. They have traditionally done so in a bid to have their own productions accepted as, well, universal. In such bids, I think *universal* signals white acknowledgment and praise, which, in my view, is nothing but slave ships all over again for the black majority. But, then, I am no genius, and here, perhaps, is no great matter.

Those almost ghostly ancestral summer moments with Mr. Faulkner yielded an album, a gathering of snapshots, a collection, re-collection, and recall of a complexly defined family affair. Just as Amilcar Cabral proclaimed "all are involved, all are consumed," with respect to revolutionary African political change, so a very midwestern American Norman McClane proclaimed that regional experience forms the bedrock of the world: "and a river runs through it."

In the reflections that follow, I speak of the river—our common and necessary convergence of black and human sympathies—as "the flow." My reflections may not make as much sympathetic sense to some as to others, but that is the price for choosing to travel with Faulkner as "family." It is a complicated business. But on a personal note that is a harbinger of what is to follow, I can say that, after the rain, the crows disappeared. Our son became saner, happier, and more stable. My writing, and my southern family geographies, arose shining from the darkened critical horizons of North Carolina with the brightness of a new day. You are welcome to walk in this twilight (or, in the terms of W. E. B. Du Bois, the illumination provided by the "birth of a new day") with me. You are welcome as a critical and remembering reader in the home this book hopes to provide for a new southern studies. You are welcome to the family—in the most comprehensive imaginable sense of the word—to a community of interests, ideas, ideals, and global concerns that may well change the common definition of America in the not-too-distant future of American life and letters.

I Don't Hate the South

On the Distinction of "Jr."

GEOGRAPHIES OF MY FATHER NAME

I am eleven years old, giddy with the joy of elemental fire and awed by the apparent invulnerability of my father. He is removing dead coals from the glowing bed of the furnace. He is risking the peril of flames. We are sharing, I think, in the heroism of taking care of the family. We are together. He is intense, sweating slightly across the brow. He still wears the shirt and tie from another long day's work. For some reason, prompted by the pure spirit of being, I begin to move. I start dancing around the furnace room with light abandon. My voice slides up the scale to a high falsetto. Some primitive god of fire possesses me; I feel joyful and secure. I am supremely happy and fluid. Then I am suddenly flattened against a limestone wall, bolts of lightning and bright stars flashing in my head. I have been hit hard, viciously slapped in the mouth. A thunderous voice shouts: "Damn it! Houston Jr., stop acting like a sissy!"

Having heard my falsetto chant, my father had turned from the furnace with the quick instinct of an exorcist. He hit me with the fury of a man seeing a ghost. The smell of wood-burning fireplaces in winter is what I recall as I ran up the basement stairs and out into a cold Louisville, Kentucky, night, astonished at how much I had angered my sacred and invulnerable father, whose moods of manhood were as unpredictable as the San Andreas fault.

My name contains the sign of ownership and descent appropriate to the bourgeoisie. I am not a second or II. I am a junior, or Jr. (junior, adj. 1. Younger. Used to distinguish the son from the father of the same name, and written after the full name). The inheritance that passes to me from Sr.—the man at the furnace—remains a mystery seasoned by small details.

The cryptic, unreadable nature of my father's life appears before me like scar tissue, with a strange and simultaneous attraction and repulsion. I want to turn away from his wounds, the scars, and the disorder I believe ripped his consciousness and shredded his boyhood days. But I cannot turn away. With each new revelation or additional detail supplied by my mother, even into her eighties, or by my brother, now in his sixties, my attention is more firmly riveted. My head and gaze are fixed like Winston's in Orwell's *1984*. I see the pain coming, but am never certain where it will fall.

⁝⁝

He was born in Louisville to a mother whose entire life was spent as a domestic for white families. His great-grandmother had escaped (or so the story was told) from a Mississippi slaveholder. She made her way to Kentucky with her owner in hot pursuit. My father's father (my paternal grandfather) was so light-skinned he might easily have been mistaken for the white slaveholder from whom my great-great-grandmother escaped. Harry was my paternal grandfather's name, and his greatest talent (or so I was led to believe) was fishing.

Prostitutes were a successful and unashamed business for my father's grandmother. From my father's boyhood perspective, his grandmother's "girls" must have seemed uncanny citizens of a bizarre extended family. I vaguely remember him telling me one day, in a faraway voice, that his first sexual encounter was with one of his grandmother's girls, who in effect raped him.

So much is difficult to turn away from in what I perceive to be the scarring of my father's life. His mother urging him to stay forever her own "good Negro Christian boy" yet regaling, tempting, titillating him with tales of the glory of white success, of spartanly clean windows, shining cars, and infinite spaces of white opportunity in America. His father hunkered down in an old leather chair, with the radio playing popular songs, dozing off after a hard day's labor in the middle of some urgent question his son was trying to ask. Reverend Sheppard, a messiah of a missionary and a boxing coach, urging those black Presbyterian boys of Grace Church to self-extermination for the glory of God and the good health of a "Negro race" that white American insurance companies would not even consider as clients.

Houston Sr.'s answer to the aching incoherence of his boyhood was summed up in an exhortation he barked at my brothers and me if he ever found us on the brink of tears. "Be a man!" There was nothing, mind you, ethnic or racial in this. Just, "Be a man!"

I remember no stories from my father's lips about being comforted in the arms of his mother or being told fuzzy bedtime stories by his father. Thus, I assume Houston Sr. was like the children of Dickens's Mrs. Jellyby. Mistress Jellyby's kids just "tumbled up." This process translates in Afro-America as "jes grew." Of course, it is true that those other children—the children of the white employers and patrons for whom my paternal grandmother and grandfather labored—probably have quite other impressions of the ersatz parental caring bestowed by Harry and his wife, Susie. In this, one is reminded of Toni Morrison's *The Bluest Eye*, a novel in which the black Pecola's mother as maid and servitor to a golden white child gives more love to her employer's bright daughter than to her own child. This dynamic, one thinks, is a peculiarly black southern domestic's tale.

Houston Sr. was left on his own to formulate commandments for his life. There were no tender mercies from parents or burning-bush epiphanies from mountaintops. "Be a man!" Only the most tightly self-controlled and unbelievably balanced postures could ensure a journey from can't to can. There was no time or space for sentimentality, tears, flabby biceps, or illness. My dad set a stark image of American conquest before himself. His notion of success was as deadpan and puritanical as the resolutions of Scott Fitzgerald's Gatsby. Houston Sr.'s code was every bit as full of cowboy morality, gutsy goodwill, and trembling guilt about treating one's parents better. Mental control was like sexual control in my father's vision; it was a kind of coitus interruptus expressed in maxims like "illness and pain are all in the mind," "a woman should never make a man lose control," "race has nothing to do with merit in the United States," "the successful man keeps himself mentally, physically, and spiritually fit." Manhood for my dad was a fearless, controlled, purposeful, responsible achievement. And its stoutest testimony was a redoubtably athletic body combined with a basso profundo for speaking one's name—especially to white folks. "Hello," he would growl in his deepest bass. "My name is Baker—*Houston A. Baker!*" I often step back and watch and hear myself in the presence of whites—especially those who overpopulate the American academy—growling like my father. "Hello, I'm Houston A. Baker, Jr.!"

If Houston Sr. had a notion of heaven, I suspect he saw it as a bright, modern building where his own well-lit and comfortably furnished office was situated next to the executive suite of Booker T. Washington. Washington's manly singleness of purpose and institutional achievements were taught to my father. He absorbed them while putting himself through West Virginia State College under the mentorship of the great John W. Davis. Houston Sr. and Booker T.—building a world of American manhood, service, progress, and control. Houston Sr. and Booker T.—in their lives of service becoming swarthy replicas of idealized white businessmen like Carnegie and Vanderbilt the elder.

And like Booker T.'s paradise of Tuskegee, Alabama, Houston Sr.'s heaven would surely have housed wives tending children who, if they were male, would be vigorously instructed to "Be a man!" When not tending children, wives would be satellites of manly Negro enterprise, raising funds and devoting body and soul to the institutional growth of a world designed by and pleasing principally to men. In my father's heaven, there would certainly be no confusion between love and sex, race and achievement, adults and children, men and not-men.

▪▪

With the household furnace billowing smoke and ash on that evening long ago, my father must have suffered the fright of his life when he heard my youthful falsetto and turned to see my lithe dance accentuated by the whitewashed walls and the glow of flames. Houston Sr. could only, I think, have grasped this scene as the perverse return of his own arduously repressed boyhood—a boyhood marked by Louisville East End economies and Reverend Sheppard's muscular Christianity. The West End, by contrast, was colored by his mother's ambivalent love for her light-skinned progeny. Houston Sr. struck out in a flash against what he heard and saw as my demonic possession by haunting fields of unmanliness. What after all could God be thinking if he had somehow bequeathed to Houston Sr. a sissy instead of a son? And so my father hit me very hard. Walking in the woodsmoke air that cold evening (actually just around the corner and through a back alley since I didn't dare stay out too long), I could not get a handle on what precisely I had done to make Houston Sr. so angry.

Years, and years, and years later, I learned the term *homophobia* . . . and labeled my father's actions accordingly. And as I think about that violent moment long ago, I realize my father was indeed afraid. Yet his fear was not nearly as simple or clearly defined as an aversion to physical, emotional, or even intense and romantic love between men. There is a strong part of me that knows my father was fascinated by and even attracted, with a level of deep admiration, to what he believed (with great earnestness) to be the intellectual superiority and discipline of what he called "the homosexual lifestyle." I think what terrified him on that evening years ago, then, was not homosexuality as he ideally conceived it. Rather, he was afraid that I was fast approaching adolescence and had not found what he deemed the controlling voice of American manhood. Clearly, therefore, it was time for Houston Sr.—he knew this with both fierce dismay and instinctive terror—to busy himself with the disciplining of Jr. The tragic emotional shortcoming of that evening was that my father did not realize that the letters at the end of my name were not meant to confirm his ownership or responsibility with respect to my name.

Jr.—as its formal definition makes abundantly clear—is meant to distinguish a younger self from the wounds of the father. It is sad that my father failed to realize that it was precisely the feelings of assurance, security, protection he had bestowed that overwhelmed me, made me want somehow to dance for him. It has required many hours of painful thought since that moment at the furnace to extract and shape for myself a reasonable definition of life in relationship to my father's Sr. and seniority.

For decades I have sought patterns to fulfill a Jr.'s life. Mercifully, I have found some. They include so very, very much that my father was forced to ignore, deny, reject, or misunderstand. He could never, for example, have given approval to the informal definition of sissy that is sisterhood. Tragically, he never envisioned a successful man's life as time measured by and defined through its intimate (if always incomplete) understanding, sharing, and comprehension of women's joys, dangers, voice, and solacing touch—shaped definitively, that is to say, by sisterhood.

Unlike the Sr. produced by ordeals I have yet fully to comprehend, it is impossible for me to imagine Jr. without a strong woman's touch. I am now the middle-aged father of a quite remarkable son. And at this moment I imagine with God's grace I shall be able to live up to the standard of distinction the concluding marks of my name are meant to signify. If I do achieve such distinction, perhaps in some far-off fall twilight, my son will raise a voice in my defense, speak rhythmic words that tell of his own self-possession in a troubled world.

⁝⁝

Of course, my father, Houston Sr., set in motion the possibilities of my son's ownership of his name—a confident, rhythmic, and healthy articulation of black identity in America. My father was ever respectful of and grateful for the options represented by Harry and Susie Baker; however, he ultimately refused their options, without a second thought. Harry's janitorial job at Brown and Williamson Tobacco provided a living wage, but it was not work of the sort that would inspire a son's emulation. My grandfather left home each day dressed in a shirt and tie. He stowed his lunch in a satchel. At Brown and Williamson he put on a janitor's outfit and swept monumental factory floors through summer heat and winter cold, enveloped in the deathly sweet smell of tobacco. My grandfather never badgered Houston Sr., or his other sons, to American heights of business or academics. I am certain Pops would have been content to see my father become a dutiful Christian hewer of wood, a manly drawer of water. And grandmother Susie would not have been outraged at such an outcome. Susie would have been more than satisfied if my dad had duded himself up in crisp chauffeur's livery and gone to work for wealthy Louisville families, which, of course, was the same thing as white Louisville families. It was unpredictable in the extreme, therefore, that Houston Sr. found the energy and "farewell to you all" flair to depart for West Virginia during the 1920s in search of a college education.

He always believed—and was always fond of telling his sons—that he simply "found" the desire for college, as though sipping it from air. I can hear him. Two high school teachers received honorable mention in his saga—one history professor and one tennis coach. Overall, my father's departure for West Virginia State was a willed act of resistance to white America's expectations that black American lives will ever be nasty, brutish, and short. The rigid racial segregation and cunning legal restraints on black American hopes and ambitions during the 1920s make my father's stated motivation plausible. A stern will and an almost visionary commitment to self-discovery were certainly necessary in what amounted to a war of confrontation. Black learning mobilized against white resistance. His departure from Louisville takes on the cast both of embattlement and relief—a rigorous and bracing confrontation with white supremacy in the office of a larger and more productive black life.

Departures from urban racism were redemptive. During our childhood, my older brother and I were always happy to leave Louisville. We loved to go "to the country" to visit our grandparents (my mother's kin) in Danville, Kentucky. Danville was a farming community and a railroad center on the Louisville & Nashville line. Early in the town's history, it was home to a vast switching yard, briskly imbricated in a network of rail travel that made the United States a commercial marvel. The town's monuments and institutions include the Kentucky School for the Deaf, a fine liberal arts college, and a statue of Dr. Ephraim McDowell, who performed the first ovariotomy in America. McDowell's statue was a familiar landmark on walks my brother and I took with our grandfather. It stood in the center of a small, elegant park bearing the good doctor's name. We usually made our trips from Louisville to Danville in the winter dark of Friday evenings. My older brother and I were wrapped in blankets like mummies. Bricks heated for the three-hour drive in a heater-less car warmed our parents' feet. After dinner, we would sit in what seemed a spacious living room overseen by my maternal grandparents, John Thomas Smith and Elizabeth Smith. Houston Sr. and my mother, Viola Elizabeth, would survey the room and its owners, then shyly look at one another. It was easy for the elders to see my parents were in love. (I know that now like I know the grip of my favorite ballpoint pen.) They had traveled miraculous educational distances from the lives of Johnny and his wife.

Johnny listed his furthest year of formal education as grade four. Elizabeth, or Lizzie, refused to claim a grade level. She entered domestic service for a white family at age eight. Johnny was a craftsman. He could turn a vacant lot into a handsome homestead without a scrap of paper passing between his initial mental estimate and the last driven nail. He was a master carpenter without vocational-school training; he was a vernacular architect without portfolio. Lizzie was skilled as a seamstress and tailor, occupations she plied on her own time. Six days a week, she labored in the office of the white Dr. Jackson. She worked as receptionist, maid, cook, woman of all work for the Jackson family. Returning to her own home for an hour each day at noon, she cooked, washed clothes, and put the household in order. On Sundays—all Sundays, and all day on Sundays—there was church, Danville's Christian Church.

I remember crackling static from a magnificent console radio. It was central to the family circle in the country. My three uncles— Vance, Ashby, Webster—left Danville in their adolescence. Only Johnny, Lizzie, and our newly arrived Louisville contingent gathered around that radio's wonderfully polished mahogany. Bright dials illuminated a sculpted wooden front; music and voices issued from the embroidered mesh of the speaker. As the coal stove sizzled and groaned, we listened to drama, music, and variety shows that still

echo in my imagination. It was always freezing when my brother
and I left the living room for our beds, located just through a cur-
tained doorway. We snuggled in frosty covers and eavesdropped
until music and the conversation of adults caused us to drift off. Big
bands mixed with the vapor of our breathing. Adult talk turned to
Houston Sr.'s ambitions, Johnny's building projects, Lizzie's slipcov-
ers for Miss Irene, Viola's thesis on George Sand—and the horrors
and indignities of Negro life in America. How Harry Truman was
faring as president.

Book learning had not confused Houston Sr. or Viola about race
in America. They knew their degrees hardly made them better, or
more richly human, than the elders of the tribe. And as surely as I
can recall the pleasures of big band music on frosty Danville nights,
I know Houston Sr. held his father-in-law in profoundly high esteem. He named my older brother John Thomas, a tribute based
on father Smith's miraculous survival work, especially his savvy in
assuring books and education to all his children. I think it seemed
something of a miracle to Houston Sr. that a family like the Smiths
could actually nurture the quest for black education, leading their
children to stunning results. Viola was valedictorian of her high
school and college graduating classes. Her brother Vance was a theo-
logically trained minister; Ashby, a University of Chicago lawyer;
and Webster held a master of fine arts in drama. Where on earth did
the parental impulse for such generational drive come from?

During my father's young adulthood in the United States, the
benefits of Negro education were preached from black pulpits on
Sunday. They were expounded daily by principals of black southern schools. Negro women's clubs valorized education in countless
rounds of service and sociability. Lizzie Smith was an avid church
worker. She acted as Danville's representative to state conferences
and conventions of the Christian Church. Johnny was a deacon. He
read more than one newspaper on a daily basis. He sometimes wrote
the convention and conference speeches my grandmother delivered.
Literate church workers, abreast of the racial and educational mandates of their time, Lizzie and Johnny nurtured children in the arts
of reading and the protocols of effective public speaking. The Smiths
seized from the black community air—the public sphere of church

and clubs and benefits and socials—ideals of literacy, book learning, and higher education. They instilled these ideals in their children.

Home bookshelves in the country held encyclopedias, Horatio Alger, Camp Fire Girls, newspapers, *The Book of Knowledge*, and Paul Laurence Dunbar. Houston Sr. got the point. If father Smith had managed, so could he. Hence, the household in which I grew up was as near a replica of Johnny and Lizzie's as my father could manage. My brothers and I had built-in bookshelves crafted by John T. Smith in our bedroom. They held the writings of Langston Hughes and Mark Twain, Paul Laurence Dunbar and Geoffrey Chaucer.

American resistance to black education was a palpable fact of my father's early life. Public schools were legally segregated, and dramatically unequal. Nowhere in mainstream media or American plans for the future was there a vision of or a commitment to an effectively educated Negro race. Even the encyclopedias of which my dad was so proud imply time and again that "Negro" and formally educated "intelligence" are incompatible.

Against a bleak backdrop of institutionally racialized knowledge, my dad's departure for college might well be considered a Nietzschean act of will. Arriving at West Virginia State College, he was, ironically, given a janitorial job by President John W. Davis, to whom he said: "President Davis, I don't have any money but I'm willing to work and work hard in order to pay for education."

In general, the impulse to education as a means of black advancement caught hold in both the home life and the public lives of Negroes in America. After all, if there seemed little future in politics, business, finance, or the higher reaches of industry, why not seek educational excellence? As Houston Sr. once put it, "They can't take away what's in your mind." Education was something we could keep.

By the mid-1930s, graduate school was as common to my mother's family as Sunday morning services at the Christian Church. But because she could not study for a master of arts in French in Kentucky, Viola journeyed during her post–Knoxville College summers to Bloomington, Indiana. Kentucky's Day Law prohibited blacks from attending white colleges and universities in-state. And white graduate programs were the only ones that provided degrees and professional certifications. In a bizarre racial reversal of slavery's exportation of Negroes downriver for profit, Kentucky and other southern states actually paid qualified blacks to study in integrated programs out of state. They were paid to go up, or over, the river.

Even in Bloomington, though, segregated campus housing forced my mother to board with a local black family. Housing was easy to come by. Easier, in fact, in my mother's recounting, than finding suitably challenging courses in Indiana University's summer school programs. Viola Elizabeth was genuinely the smartest kid in the class, to the bafflement of her white fellow students. They knew she was a whiz, even if they couldn't figure out what, racially, she was. A young white man blithely consented to have Viola lead him through the mysteries of French grammar, until he discovered she was not Mexican.

While my mother and her friend Arnetta, daughter of neighbors of the family Viola roomed with, were pursuing summer advancement, Houston Sr. was washing dishes and waiting tables on excursion boats or at exclusive white resorts in Asbury Park, New Jersey. Houston and Viola had not yet met. My dad and his classmates had to turn a profit during summers if they were to hold their heads respectably high on returning to West Virginia in the fall.

These summers of work in the North exposed Houston Sr. to the practices and pretensions of white America. On vacation and serviced by black bellhops, waiters, and maids, Asbury Park's summer whites often reverted to antebellum mores. My impression, drawn from Houston Sr.'s cryptic accounts, is that white Asbury Park vacationers were akin to those white tourists one encounters in the Caribbean today: well-heeled and congenially condescending.

The manners and customs of white vacationers in New Jersey sometimes spoke of money, breeding, and class distinctions of the Harvard and Princeton variety. Waldorf salads, oysters on the half shell, burgundies and sauternes became realities of my father's vocabulary. So, too, did snowy white napkins, reading for pleasure by shimmering swimming-pool light, natty casual clothes (complete with straw hat), and an imperious bearing that spurned manners that were not flawless. He learned the grace of ballroom dancing as well as the elocution of the leisure class. If whites sometimes reverted to racist antebellum condescension, then my father surely emulated, during his college summers, those culture importers of old, known as house slaves. James Baldwin speaks the truth when he suggests that blacks know far more about the house lives of whites than whites know about blacks. Blacks have always served inside the houses of whites.

It is fair to say that his college summers provided Houston Sr. with a far more sophisticated young adulthood than he could possibly have experienced in Louisville. And who knows, it was perhaps the random comments or chance conversations of vacationing white financiers that prompted him to believe that he, too, could become an American success story. Could it have been while serving frothy drinks to bored and manicured parties of whites that Houston Sr. first got word of the Wharton School of Business at the University of Pennsylvania? Pursuing a commercial course at West Virginia State, he would have been attuned to such news. But summer service among whites and their families—whole entourages taking a break from Wall Street—would have made Wharton's products and rewards as palpable to my dad as a $100 tip!

Before he was ready for Philadelphia and the Wharton School, however, my father felt he should take graduate courses in the commercial field. Kentucky forwarded his project in the same way the state aided Viola. The commonwealth paid him to pursue advanced work anywhere but at the University of Kentucky.

When my father first saw Viola during the summer of 1935 at Indiana University, she had already made good progress toward her master's degree in French. Her pride of person—enhanced by the image the mirror gave back of long dark hair, caramel skin, high cheek bones, deep-set brown eyes—was apparent. The calm haughtiness with which she ignored his sporty, Asbury Park self-confidence must have produced flashbacks. Houston Sr. could only have been reminded of insouciant, white, vacationing college girls tossing their hair indifferently by the pool. As he and his buddy Carl Forbes delayed that first potential date by extolling each other's virtues, Viola turned to Arnetta and said: "It's time to go. If we are going to the movies, we certainly don't have time to listen to all of this." They walked away, oblivious to the crestfallen, angry, and astonished

Houston Sr. As Viola said later: "He did not think he was a man to be ignored . . . so he was intrigued by me."

The Day Law was, thus, indirectly responsible for my parents' meeting. My dad lived in the type of Negro quarters often built adjacent to white schools such as Indiana University. Such residences were poor affairs—cold in winter, sweltering in summer—maintained and run by Negroes. A date—even one to the movies in Bloomington—was welcome relief from such quarters. During their first date, Viola and Houston Sr. became intrigued enough to pursue a second, then a third date, and finally an entire summer of dates, picnics, church socials, and porch-swing time.

⠶

When my father enrolled in the Wharton School in the fall of 1935, he found that even his journey north had not yielded a substantially improved set of on-campus options. At the University of Pennsylvania he could not live on campus, nor eat in the common rooms or cafeterias, nor feel safe on Locust Street. Living in the famous Negro Seventh Ward of Philadelphia, he made the walk from Bainbridge Street to Penn, crossing each day the historic South Street Bridge overlooking the early-morning boats on the Schuylkill River.

America was in the throes of the Great Depression. The racial arrangements of the country—North and South—made life depressing for all thinking Negroes. Houston Sr.'s attitude, however, was buoyant. And by the time he began classes at the Wharton School, his mood was made even lighter by thoughts of his and Viola's growing romance. She had become a full-time teacher of French at Bate High School in Danville, and (quite scandalously) she was sending Houston Sr. forty dollars a month from her modest salary. "My mother would have died if she had known," says Viola.

Some of my father's classmates were not nearly so fortunate. As we were growing up, my brothers and I heard more than once the story of one of them. Absent from class and missed by a professor who kept strict attendance, the inquiry was made: "Does anybody know the whereabouts of Mr. Martin?" (not his actual name). Sorrowfully, my father reported that Martin, a young black man from the South, had committed suicide the night before. "That's unfortunate," said the professor, "and it's really our fault. We try to screen out boys from those freshwater colleges. But every now and then, one slips through. Please turn to page nineteen of today's assignment." Another black classmate informed his black counterparts that he would appreciate it if they did not speak to him in public; he was crossing over into enemy territory—already in the process of passing for white.

When the great flood of 1937 wreaked havoc on Louisville, my father told the dean of Wharton that he was going to have to withdraw in order to return home and support his mother, who had been thrown out of work. With true magnanimity, the dean increased my father's stipend and urged him to remain and complete his degree. Houston Sr. began writing his thesis, a study of Negro mortality in the world of American insurance. Negroes, it seemed, were dying faster, earlier, and in greater numbers per thousand than whites in America. Few white insurers would even consider writing policies on Negro lives. When they did, they charged twice the price offered to whites. Outrageously, these expensive Negro policies matured at age eighty-five!

In Houston Sr.'s view, there were few alternatives to such white business ethics. Black insurance companies were too small and undercapitalized to take up the slack. Nevertheless, black companies were commended for their effort. "It is marvelous," reads his thesis, "how the small colored insurance companies manage to insure a group of practically all substandard lives and yet make reasonable profits, as well as offer employment opportunities to hundreds of persons." Houston Sr. received his master of business administration degree from the Wharton School in May of 1937. Eight members of his class who also specialized in insurance traveled to the headquarters of the Metropolitan Life Insurance Company in search of employment during the summer of 1937. Metropolitan at the time was quite active in insuring a Negro clientele. In his thesis, Houston Sr. repeatedly praises the company for its exceptional efforts to bring knowledge of modern health care to a black customer base. The black base of Metropolitan customers numbered more than two million by the mid-1930s. Eight (white) Wharton insurance graduates received jobs at Metropolitan in the summer of 1937. Houston Sr. was not hired.

::

Houston Sr. returned to Louisville a very disillusioned young man. White people could not take away what was in his mind. On the other hand, they did not have to acknowledge his mind at all, or give him a job. So my dad taught commercial courses at Louisville's Central High School. A graduate of the best business school in the United States, Houston Sr. took a post at a segregated Kentucky high school. He was assigned to teach typing to teenagers. In the summer of 1938, he drove a secondhand car to Danville. In the neatly trimmed backyard of Lizzie and Johnny Smith, he and Viola were married. Though they were spectacularly educated, they were Negroes and could not even dream of purchasing a house on their own. Lizzie and Johnny helped. They loaned the couple an $800 down payment. The marvel, of course, is that Houston Sr.'s belief in the codes and possibilities of American business remained intact. If he could not secure a place in the larger white business world, then he made up his mind to apply himself to the world of Negro insurance.

He wrote to the Golden State Life Insurance Company of Los Angeles, and the company responded. They promised a managerial job and a handsome salary. For their honeymoon, Viola and my dad traveled three thousand miles in their secondhand car to Los Angeles. Luscious palms, wide streets, and funky West Coast jazz in an expansive business district occupied by blacks dazzled them. Both blues and jazz were in plentiful supply. And there was money to be made by blacks on the assembly lines of the aircraft industry. Unfortunately, Golden State had suffered serious internal reorganization. The executive who had promised my dad a job was no longer with the company. The only post available with Golden State was "collecting a debit," which consisted of taking hard-earned dimes from working-class Negroes who would never be able to pay off their policies, policies like Metropolitan's that matured at age eighty-five. Houston and Viola made a U-turn. They headed straight back to Louisville without so much as an overnight motel break.

How did my father sustain his faith in education, maintain his commitment to the manly ideals of American success, even after his fruitless journey into the precincts of Negro business? What fearful symmetry of will and emotion enabled him to bear rejection with a smile and a slow shake of his head? (This was his public bearing in any case.) There must have been deep springs of bitterness flowing.

Religion is at least part of the answer. God had been good enough to put Reverend Sheppard in the East End and to create a Christian dean of the Wharton School, who increased Houston Sr.'s stipend during the Louisville flood. My dad was convinced that such men had undeniably been created by God—with Houston Sr.'s future in mind. But my father also felt that God's best reference letter in regard to power and belief might come from none other than John Thomas Smith. If God could parlay handicraft skills and a fourth-grade education into the magnificence of the Smith household, what couldn't God, and Houston Sr., do with a Wharton M.B.A.?

My father remained a practical Christian most of his life. But his heart and soul moved day to day on a secular track. He trusted his own formally educated and impeccably honed instincts to quickly and correctly distinguish between right and wrong—to express suitable black manners, culture, and decorum, in contrast to regressive black hooliganism and sexual excess. He had unshakable trust in his instincts. He was self-made, and he knew he was quite a man because he had escaped black southern working-class origins and, in a wide field for failure, even succeeded in acquiring the feel and substance of culture. He was an early riser, ever alert to details. He was an advocate for temperate sexuality and disciplined physical conditioning. He was hard-boiled in matters of emotion, whether Christian courtship or family crises. "Keep a cool head" was his injunction whenever the world tilted.

::

Taken together, my father's virtues made him an archetypal American male. Distinctive in color, his signal difference from his white, mainstream, cosmopolitan compeers was his earnest dedication to improving the lives of black people in the United States. His life was in large measure motivated by ethical and moral simplicity. His was an ethical innocence that would make Henry James's characters smile in happy recognition. It is Gatsby, however, as I earlier suggested, who most resembles my dad. I can imagine Houston Sr. responding like Gatsby under interrogation by Nick Carraway. When Nick alerts Gatsby, "you can't just turn back the clock and alter the past," a stunned Gatsby replies: "Turn back time? Of course you can!" And then it's Nick's turn to be stunned.

Houston Sr. honestly believed that nothing, except the weather, was beyond his firm and judicious control. Having successfully overcome temptations to laziness, excess, despair, greed, indigence, he greeted each day with utterly surprising and completely self-renewing vigor. Anger and bitterness never drove him to boring lamentations or whining self-pity. He figured that whatever God and white folks denied, he could ingeniously make, take, or finance on the installment plan. And having witnessed the example of, perhaps, God and, certainly, John T. Smith, he was convinced he could mold his sons in his own image.

We became the DNA proving ground for his formulas. We were prototypes for a black, disciplined, and wholly self-reliant American manhood. If he could polish us into mirrors, then he could say, in that awesome basso profundo reserved for white audiences: "It is good!"

But what on earth were we slated for? Our father's mission remained for a very long time a mystery. "All I require of you," he used to say, "is to make good grades and be a gentleman!" Grades were easy. But a gentleman, for our father, carried Asbury Park class imperatives and high-bourgeois black codes of conduct. Such imperatives and demands required strenuous perseverance and painfully disciplined self-fashioning. A financially secure, literarily and musically cultured, Christian, superbly coordinated athlete who knew how to navigate a sixteen-piece dinner setting: this was our father's brief definition of a gentleman. "Where," asked one of my colleagues at the University of Virginia, "did you ever learn what all of this silverware means?"

One of the overlooked burdens our father had to bear was the envy of whites. So many whites with whom he came in contact must have recognized, in a glance, that here was a black man who was clearly their superior. In addition to his educational attainments, Houston Sr. was a criminally handsome, dedicated family man with a beautiful wife and a progressive family. Such virtues surely compounded white envy. It was necessary, then, for our father to carry himself in ways that did not reveal his acute awareness of white men's envious insecurities. He could not risk losing white philanthropic support or the ability to move reasonably smoothly (for a Negro professional) around American social and political obstacles. The whites most likely to be envious were those closest to my father's level of attainment. They were the men and women fully resourced to contribute to his projects. They were "thinking" whites. And they knew that their thinking on racial matters was indisputably correct, characterizing all blacks—regardless of degrees, accomplishments, or family values—as beneath them.

Writing with the extraordinary power and emotional immediacy that were his gifts, James Baldwin presents his own stepfather as a violent, tragic, bitter victim of American racism. Like so many patriarchs and protagonists in the dark pages of Afro-American literature, Baldwin's stepfather was driven to violent madness by white supremacist orthodoxies. Even while Baldwin represents his stepfather at his worst, he cautions us not to judge carelessly. Invoking Scripture, Baldwin reminds us: "Thou knowest his fall, but thou knowest not his wrestlings!" Houston Sr. came home every evening to dinner with his wife and family. He prided himself on never breaking a promise to his children. "If I promise you something, you're going to get it." This was a scary promise, of course, in times of disciplinary action. Our father did not mutter darkly to himself like Baldwin's stepfather. Nor did our father lash out, like the Baldwin patriarch, at his children's barest mention of some modish white movie star or famous rockabilly singer like Elvis the Pelvis. Our father kept a cool head and pushed bitterness and violence as deep into the pit of his being as possible.

It is difficult to imagine what his everyday life must have been among the limp racial and supremacist philanthropies that financed Negro service occupations during the 1930s. His plan demanded both ferocious self-discipline and, I think, violent denial. Since it is hu-

manly impossible simply by will alone to banish illness, moral am-
biguity, sexual temptation, ambivalence, and the omnipresence of
evil from one's life, how my father must have suffered! Horror and
uncertainties exist, especially in black American life. To deny them is
to do violence to both the world and the self. But Houston Sr. pre-
cariously balanced self-denial and a miraculous faith in the American dream with his hard-won confidence in the infinite potential
for advancement of an educated, disciplined black self. His faith and
confidence—unlike what he willed to my brothers and me—was no
easy gift, or legacy, from a well-heated childhood home. He wrestled
the world and himself into recognizable forms.

Thou knowest his fall, but thou knowest not his wrestlings. The
slap in the furnace room long ago becomes far less an emblem of my
father's fall than a living memorial to what precisely he had to sup-
press in order to live and make a living. After the disappointments
of Metropolitan and Golden State, he declared he would never be
responsible for bringing Negro children into the world. Considering
that my brothers and I indeed made our way into the world despite
this declaration, perhaps he felt special responsibility, even a somewhat guilty responsibility. After we were labored into existence,
perhaps he felt he should mold us to a bearing at least as dignified
as his own if we were to survive America. Returning once again to
the miraculous writings of James Baldwin and humbly paraphras-
ing his best words, I can say that we three sons of Houston Sr. are
walking this treacherously threatened planet in our father's image,
and in varying degrees of good health. And we stand together in the
conviction that our mission in life is to survive, and to get our work
done on behalf of the black majority. We *are* good men, and honest
writers.

Libraries of Consciousness
PUBLIC READING AND AMERICAN IDENTITY

Reading was a lifelong habit for my father. He inundated our household with newspapers, *Reader's Digest, Barron's, Atlantic, Time, Newsweek,* scores of self- and business-help books. They burst out of his study door and flowed into the hallway, found their way into bathrooms, impeded the calm of staircases, overburdened the mailbox daily. His readings were everywhere: kitchen, living room, dining room, and den. As he grew older, he seemed driven to read more. It is true we sometimes found him napping during his designated reading time. Still, books, magazines, trade journals, and even the occasional Conan Doyle novel were his stock-in-trade. They constitute for me a literary memorial to Houston Sr.'s unending quest for self-improvement; they are headlines, as it were, of my father's habits and taste. Like ambitious generations of black Americans before and after, my father's cohort did believe: "They can't take away what's in your mind." My brothers and I were, therefore, strongly encouraged and instructed in the mental calisthenics of reading. I have a strange feeling sometimes that we were reading at birth! Certainly we were always immersed in books and periodicals, navigating our way among them even on the simplest of journeys through our house. And a sturdy, blue-backed set of the *Encyclopedia Britannica* was what decorators call the "reception piece" in our front hallway.

One of the most inventive business schemes my dad ever devised was to pay us: ten cents for each book we read. The ante was upped to twenty-five cents if we also wrote a report on the book. We were being instructed, I now know, in literacy and freedom. (*"They can't take away what's in your mind!"*) We were being placed at the locus classicus of Afro-American liberation struggles in America. In one of his most famous poetic jazz collages, the poet Langston Hughes speaks of the "Quarter of the Negro" as those geographies where black cuisine, religion, music, and literacy happen. At the center of the Quarter of the Negro in Louisville, Kentucky, and in the eyes of Houston Sr. was the Negro Public Library. (The main metropolitan, fully resourced library was, of course, for whites only.) In important ways, it seems to me that my southernness, literacy, and chosen profession are all intimately bound up with the Negro Public Library in the Quarter of the Negro. My father was surely the primary motivational speaker (and financier) on its behalf.

I remember exactly when I learned to read. My teacher was Miss Miles. I was six years old. I went from first to last word of a *Dick and Jane* reader with precision and reasonable southern elocution. However, it was not Miss Miles's response (she was used to such performances) but my parents' reaction that imprinted itself in my memory. The newly installed gas logs in our living room were lit. My father was characteristically still in the shirt and tie that were his daily uniform. My mother wore her schoolteacher's blazer and skirt. It was almost like a scene from *Dick and Jane*—minus Jane . . . and Spot. My parents' proud smiles and tight hugs were all I needed to make the connection between love and reading—and between my own love of reading and the road to revelation and self-esteem. There was no turning back. I began relentlessly reading in public.

As we traveled about Louisville and to distant cities, I read and pronounced aloud license plates, billboards, Burma Shave jingles, skywriting—there was no limit. "Make him stop," my older brother whined. But, God love them, my parents never did. By the time

I was eight years old, they even indulged my sinfulness, as I penciled monumentally fine short stories on church bulletins during the sermon. My parents never asked me to perform like a dancing bear of literacy for members of the black bourgeoisie who visited our home. But it was clear by the time I was ten years old that they *did* want returns on my reading that could only be achieved in public ways. ENTER: the public library.

At age ten, the public library was to me a cornucopia of riveting romances and heady biographies, seductive mysteries, tantalizing pioneering and western adventure novels, and mesmerizing sports stories. I was captivated by the abundance of the children's section where the books were rich, liberating, satisfying—carrying me instantly and completely away from the humdrum, gray, disciplined rituals of Louisville's segregated life. At those tables in the children's section, I slipped into fantasy and trance, imagining personal bests with the ease of a hawk lifting from the winter-barren branches of a giant oak, ascending with unimpeded ease into the clouds. And yet, since I was in public, the seemingly infinite variety of my reading was complemented by an endless variety of library occupants, who were young and old, able-bodied and physically challenged, soft and loud, bellicose and deferential. Naturally, all of the library's patrons were black, or, as we then called ourselves: colored. But oh, my goodness, what a wondrous space it was! As the Louisville Public Library Web site now recounts:

> The Carnegie-endowed "Western Colored Branch Library,"
> which opened in 1908, was the first library in the nation
> to extend privileges to the African American community.
> Many books by African American writers were included
> in Western's collection and served as the beginning of the
> [Western Branch's] present African American Archives.

On my frequent hikes to this Western Branch and archive, I crossed indisputably black territory, encountering a rich diversity of sounds, colors, structures, broken and smooth sidewalks, dereliction, poverty and excess, stylish hustlers and down-at-the-heels beggars. The paragraph from the Louisville Public Library Web site refers to this admixture of life, motion, and emotion as the "African

American community." And so it was, and so it appeared in all its manifold contrasts within the walls of the Western Branch Library at 10th and Chestnut streets.

My parents never expressed a single doubt or caution about my weekly and sometimes twice-weekly trips to the Western Branch. I could remain at the library for as long as I pleased. With such remarkable latitude on my hands, I read the books, of course, but I also became literate in the style, gossip, character, and expansive tolerance for class/color/economic difference of the "African American community" itself. Occupants and patrons of the Western Branch Library existed in a kind of absolute parity, especially in the eyes of the stern, colored lady librarians who were as quick to shush a high-styled bourgeois brown as a light-complected teenage athlete raucously full of himself. And those great and dedicated ladies were as swift to lead me to the newly acquired Davy Crockett adventure story as they were to accompany a smartly dressed senior to the *Complete Poems of Paul Laurence Dunbar*. Walt Whitman would have loved the Western Branch Library, its manifest and accessible variety, its comity, its shared songs of the manifold selves of the African American community. And, of course, what was so clearly inferable at the Western Branch Library were not only general, democratic vistas of American reading but also specifically African American and African diasporic valuations of literacy, the library, the habits of public reading as a certain path—in the designation of the great black liberation orator and writer Frederick Douglass—*from slavery to freedom*. Here is Douglass in the moment just after he heard his Baltimore master proclaim that "learning would spoil the best nigger in the world":

> When I was sent on errands [thereafter], I always took my book with me, and by going one part of my errand quickly, I found time to get a lesson before my return. . . . I was now about twelve years old . . . [and] I got hold of a book entitled "The Columbian Orator." Every opportunity I got, I used to read this book. . . . The more I read, the more I was led to abhor and detest my enslavers. (*Narrative of the Life of Frederick Douglass*, 82–84)

I do not want to commit the sin of historical presentism—that is, to make inaccurate revolutionary claims for the offices of the Western Branch Library by summoning the words of Douglass as though I, or we, understood them in the 1950s as we do in post–Black Power America. But certainly it seems appropriate that today the Western Branch is one of the more important archives of slave narratives and African American public reading in the United States. Moreover, I believe Douglass's resolve makes him what I want to call a "library of consciousness." Someone once commented that a scholar has only to read, study, and analyze the edited papers and writings of Frederick Douglass to comprehend fully the history of nineteenth-century America. I quite like this projection of black, literary public reading and consciousness as a Bibliothèque Nationale; I find it a fascinating notion with respect to literate consciousness and American identity.

In the final analysis, I think reading in public, and in public libraries, is the very founding act of what can only be called "American consciousness." I would argue that American identity formation and citizenship entitlements have always been projects situated as resolutely in the library as in the bivouacs of Valley Forge, and often, perhaps, more healthily and democratically situated in the Library of Congress than in the halls of Congress.

If the Western Branch Library in Louisville, Kentucky, offered me the rudimentary educational skills I would need eventually to acquire an understanding of African American identity and its relationship to national polity, I now realize, of course, that elsewhere in the United States, identity formation was just as surely occurring through the same process, namely, reading in public and in public libraries. There are always other stories to be told and heard.

When I explained to several people my idea for the present chapter, for example, they had their own stories to tell. At least two of them are far too compelling not to share. The first comes from the managing editor, Frances Kerr, Ph.D., of the journal for which I served as editor, *American Literature*. When Frances began to reminisce about the Beaumont, Texas, library days of her youth, I pleaded with her to write her reflections for me. I cite them here:

The public library in Beaumont, Texas, in the 1950s and
'60s, looked like a castle. Or a church in Europe. We didn't
go often. It was the Downtown Library, the Big Library, the
one you went to for large school projects, or just for the
occasional fun of it. The minute you stepped into the dark,
cool castle of books that was the Tyrrell Main Library, you
knew you were Somewhere Else. The children's room was
at the top of a marvel—a spiral staircase. On the landing
was a big glass cabinet containing the queens of Europe in
robes of satin and velvet, complete with miniature jewels.
Even as a child, I understood that the library didn't concern
the black people a couple of blocks away outside, waiting
at the bus stops. They didn't come here. There were no
water fountains labeled "Colored" here, as there were in
the grocery stores. . . . Everything was simply understood.

Then, there is the story from my friend, a community activist
and organizer, Jamie Kalven, who not so many years ago met my
wife and me at his "office" in one of the two remaining buildings
of the Chicago Housing Authority site known as Stateway Gardens.
The seven buildings that once comprised Stateway Gardens—along
with twenty-eight public housing towers known as the Robert Tay-
lor Homes—have now been demolished. The demolition process
was labeled "transformation" and "relocation." But what essentially
took place in a two-mile stretch along State Street that once bustled
with African American community life and culture was a clearance,
equivalent to the evacuation of blacks from Durban in South Africa
(or of poor blacks from New Orleans). The land was cleared for
"redevelopment," meaning the building, sale, and gentrification of
housing, boutiques, shops, theaters, and restaurants intended principally for white occupation and entertainment. Today, only a few
public institutions remain. One of them is the Bee Branch Library at
3647 South State Street.
    Jamie's story, as it appeared in his Web-based publication, *The View
from the Ground* (www.viewfromtheground.com), is a library story. Its
principals are Morton Walker, a black man whose conviction for
sexual assault was overturned by the Illinois Supreme Court, and his

homeless friend Shawn Baldwin, both of whom were daily patrons of the Bee Branch Library. Morton and Shawn used to meet every day at the library, where they signed up for computer terminals. They used the Internet to receive and send e-mails, look for jobs, and get a handle on the world's happenings in a warm environment. All of that changed in January 2003. Here is how Jamie describes matters in the first of his three articles devoted to the State Street Coverage Initiative:

> En route to the library the morning of January 7, Morton had an encounter with the police. He and a friend, Shawn Baldwin, were walking on State Street, when an unmarked police car driving on the sidewalk outside the grocery store at 37th approached them. Three plain-clothes officers got out and ordered them to put their hands on the car. One officer checked their IDs, while the other two searched Morton and Shawn. The officers, Morton later learned, were from the Special Operations Section of the Chicago Police Department.
>
> When Morton inquired why they had been stopped, one of the officers told him that: "There'll be no more standing on State Street. Go over to Federal, if you want to hang out." Later in the afternoon of January 7th Morton and his friend Shawn stepped outside of the Bee Branch Library to share a cigarette. The same gang of Chicago policemen rolled up on them, "ordered them to put their hands up against the wall, and handcuffed them."
>
> Morton and Shawn were charged with disorderly conduct.

The View from the Ground's subsequent reporting reveals that it was Chicago's Mayor Richard Daley himself who launched the State Street Coverage Initiative. The mayor seems to have felt that the presence of black people would be discouraging to developers.

Symbolically, the State Street Coverage Initiative can be read as simply an urban, midwestern ("out South") chapter in the book of American separation, exclusion, surveillance, and policing that have always conditioned the achievement of literacy and consciousness in the United States. We read, almost always, against the grain of public representations of civic virtue that frequently turn out to be illusions. We employ our literacy to decode so-called contested elections in America as acts of bullish theft, perpetrated by the highest court in the land, in utter complicity with oligarchic wealth. We read against the grain of mainstream media gone totally to embedded sycophancy in the camp of armed forces deploying weapons of mass destruction (yet again) against a country inhabited by nonwhites.

With such reading against the grain, all of us are libraries of consciousness bent on contesting any so-called knowledge that blocks understanding of the pathway *from slavery to freedom*. While in prison, for example, Morton Walker earned enough academic credits to be awarded a B.A. from Roosevelt University. The title of his senior thesis was "Urban Renewal: A Minority Nightmare."

Alas, for our own era, notions of libraries and reading in public as sites of reading against the grain seem to have been sharply compromised. Much has been lost or come under threat for public reading since my early days at the Western Branch Library. The draconian PATRIOT Act contains provisions that have been contested by all who—like Jamie and Frances, Morton and Shawn—are card-carrying members of the best libraries of our towns, cities, and universities in America. I will conclude this chapter with this Web site posting:

Book and Library Community Statement Supporting the Freedom to Read Protection Act (H.R. 1157)

May 15, 2003
Our society places the highest value on the ability to speak freely on any subject. But freedom of speech depends on the freedom to explore ideas privately. Bookstore customers and library patrons must feel free to seek out books on health, religion, politics, the law, or any subject they choose, without fear that the government is looking over their shoulder. Without the assurance that their reading choices will remain private, they will be reluctant to fully exercise their right to read freely.

Section 215 of the USA Patriot Act threatens bookstore and library privacy. FBI agents do not need to prove they have "probable cause" before searching bookstore or library records: they can get access to the records of anyone whom they believe to have information that may be relevant to a terrorism investigation, including people who are not suspected of committing a crime or of having any knowledge of a crime.

The lives of Frederick Douglass, Frances Kerr, and Morton Walker demonstrate that public reading is always a reading—implicit or otherwise—of the public sphere. It is an act of consciousness; it is an indispensable freedom that no matter how robustly and vigorously suppressed will always break out, as it were, into redemption songs and acts of proud revolutionary (to use Stuart Hall's word) "identification." Let reading reign!—in public by a public whose rights of privacy are secure. As an old Louisvillian and southerner, I say: Let reading reign as an efficacious act of consciousness serving to make truth a sustainable script in the American public sphere. I think back to my father, my hours at 10th and Chestnut, and I know that cherished civic freedom and responsibility are finally what it means to read in public. For Houston Sr., reading was not only a lifelong, but also a life-sustaining habit. He gave me reading, and the profit on it is that I teach and call upon any who believe I am fit to tutor, to read against the grain.

A Book of Southern Distinction

THE SOULS OF BLACK FOLK AT 100

Who can hold a telescope to history? Who can tune into the magical plasma screen and see clear details and sharp outlines of the future? I have had only two "psychic readings" in my life. Both occasions were a lark, late on city evenings, and proved completely (with apologies to Dionne Warwick) bogus. Or, in the inimitable phrasing of my nine-year-old grandson, Marquis: "bootleg." I have never consulted with a real conjure woman or conjure man. My good friend and the Louisiana poet laureate, Brenda Marie Osbey, would probably say: "Well, Houston, if you went to a white, street-corner psychic, after a bit too much red wine, what do you expect?!" Nevertheless, I am amazed that my father's injunctions and my own journeys of discovery in the world of books and reading seem to have "predicted"—with fortunate southern resourcefulness—my future. Not only did the Louisville Western Branch Public Library set me up for my choice of an English major at Howard University, but it also put me aboard a westbound airliner to Los Angeles for graduate study in what was then simply called *English*. My present occupation is clearly that of a salaried reader and teacher of books. When

I decided to devote my reading to Afro-American literature and culture, I first encountered a book of remarkable southern distinction that changed the way I thought and continue to think about, well, everything.

In graduate school at the University of California at Los Angeles, I specialized in English Victorian literature. Then I began to read black literature, and that is when I discovered W. E. B. Du Bois's *The Souls of Black Folk*. It is a southern book written by a New England black genius. During my youth, New England was to me little more than a mysteriously seductive enthusiasm of my father. He had never lived or worked in New England. Yet like Du Bois, as I shall soon explain, my father thought of New England landscapes and mores as perhaps more perfectly American than the segregated territories of the South. The influences of my early southern years and of my career as an Afro-Americanist are linked inseparably to my father and Dr. Du Bois. I consider them both valued ancestral American icons.

❖

Any account of W. E. B. Du Bois's life and work that fails to note the importance of New England as an ideological and regional influence is, ipso facto, a failure. The ideals of Du Bois and of New England converge at so many points with respect to informed labor and democratic self-reliance that the duo seems uncannily to mark an alternative black modernity in America. I remember my own youth under the tutelage of a father who sometimes thought like Du Bois. (Although, as earlier discussed, there can be no doubt that he imbibed Booker T. Washington, he was *instructed* in Du Bois.) Certainly, Houston Sr. set great store by New England—even though he (like Washington) was a southerner through and through. When my older brother and I reached adolescence, our father took the initiative to introduce us to a world beyond our hometown, beyond segregated southern school systems, beyond austere provinciality.

He chose summer camps in Williamstown and Springfield, Massachusetts, for us to attend, so that we might experience firsthand a different racial atmosphere in the Berkshires' effluvium of America's representative men and Yankee sympathies. He prodded our adolescent selves out of the swampy segregationist vapors below Mason and Dixon's line in order to transport us to a better place. On one long road trip to carry us to summer camp in New England, a Massachusetts state trooper stopped us—flashing red lights, siren, and all that jazz. Since the year was 1953, do I need to add that the trooper was white? In any case, the trooper was efficiently polite, but anxiously curious. "Don't they have summer camps in Kentucky?" he asked my dad. "Why are you bringing your boys all the way up here to camp?" "Officer," said my dad, "can I talk to you for a minute?" "All right," responded the trooper, as my dad carefully opened the door and stepped out of the car. Our father and the officer began to exchange words in low voices, and before we knew it they were strolling back to the officer's vehicle in casual conversation.

Our dad was back there for almost twenty minutes, and then we saw him shake hands with the trooper, who got into his car and drove away. Dad got back into our car. By then we were in a state of suppressed frenzy, having made up childish horror stories about being taken to jail, clapped into "juvy," or hung. "What happened?" "What did he want?" "What were you doing?" "What were you talking about?" We bombarded Dad with questions. "Well," said Dad, "he asked me why I was bringing you all to New England to camp. He also said I was speeding, and I had to talk to him." "What did you say?" Without blinking an eye, Dad said: "I told him I wanted my sons to experience a place where not all white people acted evilly, especially white policemen. I told him New England was the best." Our dad did not get a ticket, and I have been quietly grateful to New England ever since for that wily, road-trip racial convergence of North and South.

My dad's faith in the "anti-evilness" and civic virtues of New England mirrors the faith in the Berkshires and their democratic vistas found in the writings and propinquities of W. E. B. Du Bois. The great sage describes his birthplace as "the hills of New England, where the dark Housatonic winds between Hoosac and Taghkanic to the sea." During long and brilliantly productive days, Du Bois repeatedly turned to New England models—whether famously democratic town meetings, or the stalwart academic excellence of Harvard—in his quest to outline a "good life" for the black Ameri-

can majority, and indeed, for America as a whole. Du Bois believed
his own sternness of character and rigor of method were direct
products of a "New Englandness" captured by the poet who said
of New Englanders: "They love a cross for them to bear." In *Dusk
of Dawn*, his famous "Autobiography of a Race Concept," Du Bois
writes: "In general thought and conduct I became quite thoroughly
New England. It was not good form in Great Barrington to express
one's thoughts volubly, or to give way to excessive emotion. We were
even sparing in our daily greetings" (19). Spare, serious, focused is
one way to translate the phrase "a cross for them to bear."

::

New England does not wholly contain, however, the multitude of
Du Bois's experience. He was as much at home in rural Tennessee
schoolhouses and in Manhattan boardrooms of the National Association for the Advancement of Colored People. He was as much at leisure sipping Rhine in Heidelberg as he was savoring groundnut stew
in Accra. He moved with the same purposeful stride in Monrovia
that he later brought to Moscow and Beijing. He was a cosmopolitan genius, even if New England was his default locale. And it was
perhaps only New England that could have bestowed upon him—a
bright-skinned African American man born during the tumult of
southern Reconstruction—the necessary tools and chutzpah to
dedicate his life so fervently and implacably to a difficult cause. On
his twenty-first birthday, in his tiny cell of a room at Harvard, Du
Bois constructed his version of an altar. Kneeling before its flickering
candlelight, he pledged his intellect, soul, and sacred honor to the
Herculean task of raising the status and condition of "the American
Negro" in world esteem *during his lifetime*. He never wavered from this
vow of his youth. Du Bois committed himself at age twenty-one,
in deeply dramatic and highly rhetorical prose, to a quest that he
pledged as follows:

> The hot dark blood of the black forefather born king of
> men is beating at my heart, and I know I am either a genius
> or a fool. Be the Truth what it may I will seek it on the pure

assumption that it is worth seeking—and Heaven nor Hell,
God nor Devil shall turn me from my purpose till I die.

Du Bois traveled globally, questioned universally, studied end-
lessly every conceivable source of wisdom in his quest for his silver
fleece: the elevation of the black races of the world to esteemed
recognition and expanded life chances. Despite the global reach of
his self-assigned mission, Du Bois was always committed to a local
American focus: the Negro in the United States and, principally,
in the South. The great twentieth-century black author Richard
Wright proclaimed: "The Negro is America's metaphor." Du Bois
focuses precisely on the part-for-whole, metaphorical relationship
of the Negro to America that Wright proclaims. The "Sage of Great
Barrington" (as Du Bois came to be called) states his theme like a
virtuoso jazz musician, locating his life's vocation in long melodic
phrases that become his own uniquely multifaceted riff:

> The problem of the twentieth century is the problem of the
> color-line: the relation of the darker to the lighter races of
> men in Asia and Africa, in America and the islands of the
> sea. It was a phase of this problem that caused the Civil War;
> and however much they who marched South and North in
> 1861 may have fixed on the technical points of union and
> local autonomy as a shibboleth, all nevertheless knew, as
> we know, that the question of Negro slavery was the real
> cause of the conflict.

As with all great jazz, Du Bois's phrasing is scintillating. It pro-
vocatively allies a global universal ("the problem of the twentieth century") with a specific, inescapable, and contemporaneous
American dilemma ("the question of Negro slavery"). Decades
before Gunnar Myrdal labeled it (and certainly with far more poetry), Du Bois set a mighty research agenda for American race relations. He predicated a universal American "problem" as embodied
in precisely the history and condition of the Negro in the United
States. He explicitly claimed that America and its racial dilemma
(and the great and devastating Civil War, in which nearly 600,000
soldiers, North and South, perished) provide an apt case study for

pivotal questions of twentieth-century global relations. He claimed, in brief, that the modernity of the "human sciences" was ineluctably contingent upon proper answers to inescapable questions of "race" in the United States. He, thus, took on imperialism, colonialism, and grand questions of power and difference, by situating them not only in the context of America but also in the domain of American race relations, as they could be read from a distinctively southern United States polity. We turn to the opening of chapter 9 of *The Souls of Black Folk* and hear the following:

> The world-old phenomenon of the contact of diverse races of men is to have new exemplification during the new century. Indeed, the characteristic of our age is the contact of European civilization with the world's underdeveloped peoples. Whatever we may say of the results of such contact in the past, it certainly forms a chapter in human action not pleasant to look back upon. War, murder, slavery, extermination, and debauchery—this has again and again been the result of carrying civilization and the blessed gospel to the isles of the sea and the heathen without law. . . . [in the future] "the survival of the fittest" in culture contact must mean "the triumph of the good, the beautiful, and the true." . . . It is my present task . . . to indicate how *the black race in the South* meet and mingle with the white in . . . matters of everyday life. (my italics)

We do well, I think, to interpret Du Bois's mission statement as the claim that the condition of black folk in the American South offers a material, empirical, and intellectual laboratory for studies in global relations in culture contact and human difference. His famous Atlanta University Studies, of which he alone composed more than two thousand pages, were meant to investigate critical areas of black life on ten-year cycles for one hundred years by collecting and scientifically analyzing carefully secured sociological and ethnographic data. The "look" of Du Bois's achieved method and work can be readily inferred from his magisterial work *The Philadelphia Negro*.

The South that Du Bois portrays in *The Souls of Black Folk* is a land fraught with turn-of-the-nineteenth-century conundrums, dilemmas, and unequivocally material problems of modernity—"modernity," that is to say, read in terms of black labor, its conditions of leadership, and fruitful prospects for a twentieth-century future. For Du Bois deems economics, politics, and human prejudice inseparable as he seeks to analyze the post-Reconstruction South and to provide an emancipatory agenda for the life and labor of the southern black majority. Poetically and intellectually, he paints a rich canvas of a mythical South—both half-perceived and half-created by his own creative/scholarly imaginings. Du Bois's "story" is, thus, a southern metaphor for the "march of white civilization" through global territories of color. It surely bears expository resemblance—in its rich, lyrical, analytical complexity—to the classic jazz masterpiece *We Insist! The Freedom Now Suite*, composed and orchestrated by the famous black percussionist Max Roach, with brilliant collaboration by vocalist Abbey Lincoln and saxophonist Coleman Hawkins. Roach's jazz suite is in seven parts, recapitulating African and African diasporic struggle, journeying, and liberation movements in sound. Du Bois's *Souls* could have served as inspiration for such mythically proportioned, jazz historical tonalities. No one who has ever heard *The Freedom Now Suite*, or astutely read Du Bois' *Souls*, can forget that the Negro is America's metaphor.

::

The Souls of Black Folk was recognized from its first publication as a work of unique genius. After receiving a copy from his brother William, the great American novelist Henry James declared Du Bois's expository suite: "the only Southern book of distinction published in many a year." Generations of Afro-American intellectuals, creative writers, and artists have designated *Souls* one of the most important, influential, and insightful works Afro-American expressive culture has produced. The towering effects of *Souls* are the result, at least in part, of its diversity and grand ambitiousness. The scholar Arnold Rampersad points out that Du Bois's masterpiece is composed of an array of forms and rhetorical styles. It broadcasts the sage as poet, prophet, and polemicist. Rampersad writes:

> If all of a nation's literature may stem from one book, as Hemingway implied about *The Adventures of Huckleberry Finn*, then it can as accurately be said that all of Afro-American literature of a creative nature has proceeded from Du Bois' comprehensive statement on the nature of the people in *The Souls of Black Folk*. (89)

Because *Souls* is such a foundational text of the Afro-American intellectual tradition, it seems appropriate to categorize Du Bois as the inspiriting groundbreaker and enduring intellectual repository for the study and understanding of black cultural life in America. And the land of black root-and-branch on which *Souls* takes its stand is, as already suggested, the *South*. Once again, Henry James: "the only book of Southern distinction published in many years."

Where then, should we focus if we wish to understand the South and the life of the southern black majority that Du Bois so magnificently portrays in *The Souls of Black Folk*? I think our focus must be what Du Bois himself calls the "modern democratic self-reliant laborer." This model of citizenship suggests for Du Bois an enormously productive and empowering role for the millions-strong black workforce that, when he wrote *Souls*, was abjectly tilling soil south of the Mason-Dixon.

However, I believe that Du Bois also means to aggregate under the phrase *modern democratic self-reliant laborer* a number of the arrangements and formations that we have come to think of as modernization. Though his formulation seems economically driven (labor) and thus foreshadows the later Marxism of *Black Reconstruction*, "modern" for Du Bois signifies a new cosmopolitan circuitry of capital, goods, and ideals. He is concerned to strike decisive ideological, expository, and (in utopian hope) global policy blows against a colonialism that requires subservient, violently policed provinciality and abject labor to make its projects feasible and profitable. When Du Bois speaks of "self-reliant," he is surely moving to the drumbeat of Emersonian, New England, transcendental ideals that pledged their faith and intuition to the spiritual energy of the universe for the production of men of genius. Du Bois was convinced that the most talented men among black Americans had far outgrown what he calls a "credulous race childhood." In "Self-Reliance," we hear Emerson proclaim:

> And we are now men, and must accept in the highest mind the same transcendent destiny; and not minors and invalids in a protected corner, not cowards fleeing before a revolution, but guides, redeemers, and benefactors, obeying the Almighty effort, and advancing on Chaos and the Dark.

Rooted in dignified labor for the black majority (worldwide), Du Bois's self-reliant modernism is meant to advance prophetically on the chaos and darkness of colonialism, color-line subjugation; it is meant, as well, to transform and put in commerce the undeniably unique spiritual gifts of the best that has been thought, known, and sung by those who lived within the vale. An "African America" of dignified labor, fluid cultural exchange, and anti-imperialist sentiment would go a long way, Du Bois believed, toward global modernization. Converting this black abject workforce of the South into modern, democratic, self-reliant labor was a first step toward such an ideal.

Souls, with its reigning metaphor of the all-dividing vale, makes clear from the outset that there *is* a seemingly insurmountable gap between the narrator's vision of black, liberated, democratic labor and the blood-stained, brutal racial realities of postbellum southern life. Du Bois writes in "Of the Sons of Master and Man":

> [Black working men] have been trained for centuries as slaves. They exhibit, therefore, all the advantages and defects of such training; they are willing and good-natured, but not self-reliant, provident, or careful. If now the economic development of the South is to be pushed to the verge of exploitation as seems probable, then we have a mass of workingmen thrown into relentless competition with the working men of the world, but handicapped by a

training the very opposite to that of the modern self-reliant democratic laborer. (323)

The great indebtedness of the American South—and of the federal "victors" over the South in the Civil War—resides in a grand
American failure to provide for some four million black working men
and working women left emancipated, but entirely unresourced, by
the Civil War. No "fine-spun theories of racial differences," writes
Du Bois, are needed "to prove the necessity of . . . *group* training after
the brains of the [Negro] race have been knocked out by two hundred and fifty years of assiduous education in submission, careless-
ness, and stealing" (323; my italics). In a word, the South, and the
country at large, effectively abandoned the black emancipated millions, leaving them without training, land, money, or technology.

⁑

The South that Du Bois finds when he journeys from his model New
England home on the Housatonic to Fisk University in Nashville,
Tennessee, is a land of sharp separations between black and white
with respect to modernity. Whole archives and giant portfolios of
wrongheaded notions about the proper kind of leadership and training guide this South and withhold valuable resources the black majority requires in order to move into the light of an evolving modern
world. In a sense, the motivating question of *The Souls of Black Folk* is:
What distinctively southern Marshall Plan can be implemented to
raise the black majority to the status of "modern self-reliant democratic laborer[s]"? This, of course, was a national question as well because there would be no real union between North and South until
the status and condition of the Negro (over 90 percent of whom lived
in the South) was adequately addressed—a process that, in all its lan-
guishing "deliberate speed," has dragged from post-Reconstruction,
to the civil rights victories of the mid-1960s, to the devastating
scourge of Hurricane Katrina in 2005.

    It is quite accurate to call *The Souls of Black Folk* a southern, postwar
book, striving to map a plan of modernity and economic self-
reliance for the black majority. The distinguished black book appeals

to both the sectional and national interests of those who made up what Du Bois calls the "best white . . . public opinion." It is those "best whites" who must be convinced that the conversion of the Negro from "mule of the world" to democratic laborer will bring "untold assets to the American polity."

Souls brings to its mission in modernity, and national racial recognition, all the riffs in the rhetorical arsenal of the young Fisk-Harvard-and-Heidelberg-trained intellectual, W. E. B. Du Bois. It rewrites a traditional southern history of chivalrous, cavalier planters and brainlessly happy slaves. Drawing upon demography, sociology, archival research, and a deeply informed consciousness of the story of African labor in the New World, *Souls* imagines a southern past of colonizing and brutal exploitation of men, land, and labor by "white civilization," like that which pines today to come home from the spreading of democracy in, say, Iraq. *Souls* captures the all-prevailing racism of southern whites who had only the sign "nigger" to mark (as with William Faulkner's Thomas Sutpen in *Absalom, Absalom!*) the difference between themselves and those who lived "within the vale." Skin color and death are twinned realities of southern life upon the Sewanee, beside the Delta, on the rich loam of the southern Black Belt.

❖

The short story that forms chapter 13 of *The Souls of Black Folk* is titled "Of the Coming of John." It is a tale of tragic misunderstanding, brutal suppression of thought, perversion of ideals, and, finally, physical degradation and murder resulting from a southern politics and economics of racism and colonizing exploitation. His own community rejects "Black John" as a result of his transformation at the university into an intellectual savant. Meanwhile, the white world cautions Black John against conveying to his black pupils the girding ideals of modern democracy as drawn from the French Revolution. "White John," heir of the planter class, reveals himself as a descendant of a racial mentality given to what we can call white privileged purposelessness. White John believes his rights include sexual access to the black woman's body. White John's father is a judge, hence symbolizing for the story as a whole a dressed-up parody of "social justice." The black church that nurtures Black John is a mockery of rhetoric and thought. In the story, the white colonization of land and bodies represented by chattel slavery leaves a legacy of racism, black conservative collaboration with whites, social separation by Jim Crow, and quick violence. All these forestall modernity in the South. They only lead to failed ambition and tragic death. "Of the Coming of John" is an allegory of southern failure, a tale about wasting resources of young men's lives. It is a morality tale intended thoroughly to discredit old southern social arrangements of life marked by "knocking the brains out" of black laborers in the interest of white privilege.

∷

The gendered twin chapter of "Of the Coming of John" is "Of the Meaning of Progress." Cast more as memoir than fiction, "Of the Meaning of Progress" looks at the black, rural world of Tennessee through the eyes and aspirations of the exquisite, romantically represented Josie.

> It was a hot morning late in July when the school opened. I trembled when I heard the patter of little feet down the dusty road, and saw the growing row of dark solemn faces and bright eager eyes facing me. First came Josie and her brothers and sisters. The longing to know, to be a student in the great school at Nashville, hovered like a star above this child-woman amid her work and worry, and she studied doggedly. (48)

The ultimate result of Josie's commitment and longings is overdetermined by the same evils that mark the landscape in "Of the Coming of John." Describing the mind of the black majority in that rural Tennessee place where he first went for summer teaching, Du Bois says:

> The mass of those to whom slavery was a dim recollection of childhood found the world a puzzling thing. It asked little of them, and they answered with little, and yet it

ridiculed their offering. Such a paradox they could not understand, and therefore sank into listless indifference, or shiftless, or reckless bravado. (5)

From this—the indifferent black village masses—Josie stands out.

Josie is a heroic black girl/woman who cannot stand listlessness or resignation. Her "wings beat against their barriers—barriers of caste, of youth, of life, at last, in dangerous moments, against everything that opposed even a whim" (51). She takes upon herself the whole burden of support for her family—working endless hours, failing in a disappointing love affair, coming finally (like Black John) to a tragic and untimely death.

What forecloses all possibilities for Josie's soaring on the wings Du Bois bestows upon her is the material and spiritual sparseness of her world. She suffers an awful indifference to her spirit. Those who ideally might have helped to change her life do not. The southern village where Du Bois taught was a place marked by "three- or four-room unpainted cottages, some neat and homelike, some dirty," two ramshackle churches, and a sagging, sad-colored schoolhouse. This "little world," as Du Bois calls it, was, of course, a leftover, a vestige of black material deprivation and white violence. The only redemption and salvation for Josie are found at distant Fisk University. This historically black school lies an enchanted distance beyond the hills that enclose her. The brutal necessities of black subsistence living in a racist South, alas, gain the upper hand. Josie works herself to heartbroken death.

What does monetary or agricultural "progress" mean, asks Du Bois, when compared with the Jim Crow ethics of below-the-Mason-Dixon racism? "How many heartfuls of sorrow," he asks, "shall balance a bushel of wheat?" Here must be what we today call an *economics of compassion*. Such a manifestation of the heart and mind would evaluate southern needs and goals in deeply human terms, giving hope of progress to the spirit. It is something that lifts beyond backwater blues of bastardy, listless indifference, and simmering hatred bred of old wrongs and abject parochialism, to a new day—globally.

Having made his survey and beautifully recalled it in "Of the Meaning of Progress," Du Bois—with fitting dark irony—says he rode musingly back to Nashville after his Josie experience in the Jim Crow car. The devastating limitations imposed on black life and southern, national possibilities for "modernity" are nowhere more blatantly and absurdly demonstrated than in the regulated separation of black and white marked by Jim Crow. Jim Crow is the bizarre white southern hallmark of anti-progress. It is the spirit-murderer of the black majority.

What, then, are the recommendations in *The Souls of Black Folk* for shaking a retrogressive American South out of its racist slumber, giving birth to the brightness of global modernity? Du Bois recommends an informed American history, sociology, and cultural accounting of the world within the vale created by African minds and bodies snatched violently from another continent and impressed into servitude on the shores of the Americas. Out of the violence and abjection of "undemocratic" slave labor, black men and women crafted material, psychological, spiritual, and intellectual forms of life that constitute, in Du Bois's estimation, a folk culture. This culture, in *The Souls of Black Folk*, amounts to the lifeways of a black nation—a *black nation* within the larger American polity beyond the vale. Southern in its geographies, speech, religious intonation, and demographics, the black nation bears the weight of a colonial history in which the filthiest labor and most exploitative wages (when there *were* wages) fell to black "natives."

The dominantly agricultural, colonial economics of the American South (reinforced at every turn by Jim Crow laws, politics, and everyday life) blocks all efforts to count and praise the gifts of the black nation to the world. Black America's spiritual, artistic, and psychological gifts include uncanny will and perseverance in the face of deprivation and violence; improvisatory, communal formulas for "making a way out of no way"; and brilliantly expressive "sorrow songs," or "Negro spirituals." The resoluteness of will and the transformation of suffering into song by black minds and bodies that were treated like beasts of burden is worthy of our national regard. For Du Bois, they constitute a type of secret history. He thus demands both an alternative history and an alternate modernity as answers to the problem of the twentieth century: the "color line." In other words, those capable of forging national culture out of chattel slavery, and of producing a poetry as sublime as sorrow songs, must be defined not only as possessors of souls (a feature *not* accorded them by slave law and theology)—but also as resonant, richly symbolic exemplars of American democracy struggling to be born.

▪▪
▪▪

Du Bois is clear in *The Souls of Black Folk* that the power of the black nation stands everywhere suppressed, colonized, held in check by Jim Crow and those Afro-Americans who are its abettors. Black "brokers" for the white world, these abettors regard the black nation as no more than a heathen backwater to white "civilization." In Du Bois's account, black brokers are avatars of slave drivers and the assimilated and "white-minded" house servants of slavery's past. They advocate misguided, parochial, retrogressive ideology and programs for the nation. They call for an exclusively vocational/technical/normal/manual education for blacks. They urge blacks to accept Jim Crow. They are, thus, black adjuncts to a "New South" slavery for the black nation.

The *black adjunctive* is a class of black men, handsomely resourced by southern and northern white dollars, doled out to keep the black nation in its place. That place is, of course, the mudsill—those habitats such as Josie's ramshackle hamlet or, perhaps, the coffin or unmarked grave of Black John. The exemplar of the black adjunctive in *The Souls of Black Folk* is Booker T. Washington of the Tuskegee Institute in Alabama. Without shaking the hornets' nest of the age-old prisoner's dilemma of Booker T. and W. E. B., it might suffice to say that Booker T. Washington was indisputably a power-hungry broker of retrogression to the black majority.

White dollars from the North and South streamed into his hands and pockets with the speed of e-mail. He was unabashedly at the beck and call of rich white men who ran things. He brought mental, spiritual, political, psychological, and social incarceration to blacks at Tuskegee. Du Bois's monumental repudiation of Mr. Washington's "miseducation" for modernity are thunderously captured in the sage's brilliant polemic "Of Mr. Booker T. Washington and Others," chapter 3 of *Souls.*

::

Finally, what Du Bois proposes in *Souls* is the establishment of a black leadership capable of paving the southern road for the entry of a democratic, self-reliant black laborer. He calls that leadership the "Talented Tenth." The Talented Tenth, as opposed to the black adjunctive, is an informed, college-bred black elite, sharing (with, presumably, the best white public opinion) an ideal of culture derived from New England, classical in cast, but focused on southern ground.

The Talented Tenth would, in Du Bois's hopeful projections, work in harmony with white people in America to confer upon those like Josie and John "university" ideals—and degrees. This all commences, of course, to sound uncomfortably close to the bestowal of Western civilization on what Du Bois himself defines as a "partially developed people (!)" The yellow caution flag of NASCAR goes up! For, in actuality, Du Bois's recommendations for black majority progress have about them a distinct air of white-university-inspired, New England recolonization. The sage often sounds in *The Souls of Black Folk* like the colonial, ethnographically limited administrator in African novelist Chinua Achebe's classic *Things Fall Apart. Souls* sometimes displays an aloof curiosity and imperiousness of tone in the presence of the black masses. Its judgments of black humanity are frequently unduly harsh, as when Du Bois talks of the "black mob, gaudy and dirty." Du Bois unequivocally separates himself and "his house" from the black "criminal class." *How*, we want to shout at such moments of the book, *do you get off making such elitist judgments from your Harvard puritanical heights!?*

What the guiding voice of *Souls* ultimately extols, however, is the larger good of the black majority—the black nation—under a true, committed, and liberatory black leadership. We have to acknowledge the radical force of Du Bois's voice, its distinctive and courageous stance, reading against the grain of Jim Crow. We must also make due allowance for Du Bois's identifiable rhetorical exuberance and his borrowing from the reigning "civilizing" discourses of his era—discourses that certainly did not lack for colonial governors. Even a genius like Du Bois could not shake entirely free of the world historical forces that shaped his era.

⠿

The American South would do well to enter into broad collaboration with the leadership of a black Talented Tenth. That leadership would bring together—especially in education and social science—the best of two worlds. The black Talented Tenth would combine the best that had been thought, known, and said in Western civilization with the most resonantly poetic, religious, psychological, and spiritually creative gifts of the black nation. The result would be new opportunities for a new class of Americans: black citizens at large, who would, at least, be qualified as *democratic, self-reliant, enfranchised laborers.* These "new Americans," in the best case, would be welcomed as a class into large conformity and gracious harmony with a newly tolerant and racially integrative American polity. This polity would, in turn, witness a transformed South in enlightened self-interest giving up Jim Crow and committing itself fully to genuine national union.

Out of *The Souls of Black Folk*, therefore, comes a new song of the South—not one of sorrow but a rousing ballad of hope triumphant, as college-bred black leaders give birth to successive generations of university-trained graduates like Black John, imbued with ideals of the best that civilization has to offer. The work of the black intellectual would no longer fall on fallow ground. Josie—and countless Josies—could take newly conceived, entitled roles not simply as denizens of the domestic, but veritably as custodians of culture. And the black majority would in the aggregate be provided with all the resources, guidance, opportunity, and leadership needed to stand as self-reliant, democratic, modern laborers.

⠿

Thus, New England meets the postwar South in the person of a visionary black man of genius, W. E. B. Du Bois. *Souls*, which turned one hundred years old in 2003, is a magnificent southern American classic. A century ago, Du Bois offered a vision of modernity that assumed we could and would as a nation articulate the proper coordinates for a bright racial future. What is most glorious, I think, about his social, creative, and scholarly efforts is their ambitious idealism, social prophecy, and focus on the gifts of the Negro. And yet . . . what is scandalously mournful about the hundred-year-old vintage, idealistic glow of *The Souls of Black Folk* is the violent "southernness" of the United States of America today.

We exist at a time when the racial profiling, incarceration, sodomizing, assault, and murder of dark-skinned citizens everywhere is the racial norm. Louisiana, Mississippi, and Texas in the South (recently racially and class-consciously devastated by Hurricanes Katrina and Rita) hum with the spirit-and-body-murdering machinery of a private prison industrial complex and blatant federal racism and neglect. In the North, the criminal justice system, working under the thesis that a single broken window can give license to a black criminal class to vandalize and murder, has instituted "street stops," "drug sweeps," and "urban clearance" initiatives to eradicate black and brown presence in newly gentrified parks, gardens, malls, and thoroughfares. All of which gives whole new connotations to the phrase the "white city."

Did Du Bois, then, miss the mark? If racism and the criminalization, unemployment, and incarceration of the black majority are still regnant facts of American everyday life, did Du Bois fail at that pledge he made on his twenty-first birthday at his Harvard altar? To my mind, the answer is a resounding no. For books do not themselves alter reality. They simply imagine reality's change. And *Souls*, a hundred years later, still serves us memorably well in imagining, planning, and scholastically forecasting work yet to be done in and on America's twenty-first-century South. If, in fact, the Negro is America's metaphor, then certainly the South is a metonym for what went and continues to go wrong with America.

Black novelist John O. Killens enlightened us that our nation consists of three parts: down South, up South, and out South. As the South goes, with respect to race, democratic labor, and modernity, so goes our nation. And if this is true, then a book of southern distinction such as *The Souls of Black Folk* is an invaluable southern legacy. It is bequeathed to us by a man who was a New Englander at birth and, perhaps, in imaginative longing. But one who remained always a southerner in his soul(s).

Still Crazy after All These Years

A YALE BLACK STUDIES STORY

The story behind my arrival in New England as an Ivy League professor is as resonant with soundings of familial roots and distinctly southern intonations as the song of an African praise singer. When I was a twenty-four-year-old graduate student at the University of California, I telephoned my father from Los Angeles and informed him that I had been offered an opportunity to study abroad at the University of Edinburgh in Scotland. I did not want to leave L.A. My wife had just landed an amazing job as a social worker. Her territory was post–urban-riot Watts. She was earning the luxurious salary of $6,000 a year! Our combined income (including my graduate fellowship) in 1967 was nearly $10,000. Given my father's financial canniness I expected him to say: "Son, forget about Scotland." Instead, to my surprise, he said: "Oh, no, Houston, we don't pass up opportunities like this. An opportunity to experience European culture abroad is priceless. Oh, no! I'll back you if you get into financial trouble over there." So my wife quit her job. We drove nonstop to the East Coast and caught a flight to Scotland, where I, without interruptions, wrote my Ph.D. dissertation in eight months.

Meanwhile, my older brother became one of the first black lawyers on Wall Street. He justifiably landed a job at the prestigious firm of Winthrop, Stimson, Putnam, and Roberts. Some of the white chaps at his firm told him about the academic largesse of "affirmative action." If his younger brother indeed held an actual Ph.D. in English, then that younger brother should by all means seek employment at Harvard, Princeton, or Yale. As was my brother's beneficent habit, he immediately wrote me and told me what I ought to do.

Suddenly, my dad was pushing me out of the United States into thermally challenged regions of the United Kingdom; my older brother was urging me to apply for jobs at universities where blacks historically hadn't stood a chance. My wife also urged: "What have you got to lose?" Suffice it to say: I landed my first job at Yale. My Yale good fortune convinced my dad and my brother that the moral arc of the universe bends toward justice, even if it takes centuries to arrive at its goal.

What follows is a black studies story. It comes from New England. In an instant—like the blink of an eye—Du Bois's birth landscape and I were joined in unexpected camaraderie. New disciplinary formations and rampant black idealism akin to the Sage of Great Barrington's passionate dedication to racial uplift at his Harvard altar were the order of the day when I commenced work at Yale. For in the late 1960s, Yale was essentially a black studies construction site. New Haven itself was full of energy, having been designated a "model city." Radical futurists held high expectations that the next, most advanced stage of urban American life would be demonstrated in Yale's hometown. Indeed, all that might be accomplished by an urban-based black studies program at an Ivy League university was foreshadowed by the symposium on black studies organized by black Yale undergraduates in 1967. The students worked in coalition with influential university administrators and in collaboration with well-financed allies like the Ford Foundation to plan the symposium. But since there were scarcely enough African American undergraduates at Yale to fill even a single oversized classroom, the symposium was a very select and elite gathering. Its proceedings were published under the title *Black Studies in the University*.

By the time my wife and I became residents of New Haven in 1968, a number of constituencies seemed eager to transform the best wisdom of the symposium into a real academic program. Stunningly, I was invited to serve on the Yale black studies planning and advisory committee, chaired by the eminent anthropologist Sidney Mintz, who went on to cofound the famous Department of Anthropology at Johns Hopkins University. The invitation to join the committee was surprising for at least two reasons: I was only twenty-five, and I had absolutely no black studies expertise or experience. My dissertation was titled "The Idea in Aestheticism" and featured analyses of nineteenth-century English Victorian poets dedicated to "art for art's sake."

During my graduate days in Los Angeles, I had a classmate named Addison Gayle, Jr. Addison had marched, debated, and socialized with a variety of New York leftists (black, white, and Puerto Rican) during his undergraduate years at the City College of New York. He had studied black literature with James Emanuel, and was bent on writing his master's thesis on J. Saunders Redding's memoir, *On Being Negro in America*. When I met Addison, he was busily shaping (in the great American vein of self-invention) a persona as a black, pipe-smoking, tweed-wearing, eastern seaboard–living, existential intellectual, sojourning among western provincials for a season. "Why, Ole Man," he said to me, "you *cahn't* even get the Sunday *Times* delivered to your door in this God-forsaken place!" He was originally from Newport News, Virginia—and trying systematically to forget it. Ten years older than I, and a mega-fast reader, he became perhaps the most respected and admired critic of the "black aesthetic" of the 1960s. He seemed in 1965 Los Angeles a serious and suitable mentor for a country boy like me, still bearing, like an organ grinder's accordion, my cacophonous Kentucky accent. Addison told me what black books to read, steering me to James Baldwin and LeRoi Jones, Richard Wright, and, of course, Saunders Redding. He was sternly didactic about the responsibilities of black intellectuals in the United States. And he was my only "personal trainer" in anything that might remotely be called black studies prior to my arrival at Yale. So, I did seriously (having accepted the invitation to be on the planning committee) need to prepare myself to serve. I needed to learn more.

Little did I realize my angst and seriousness might have been allayed if I had spoken immediately upon arrival with the chap who occupied the Branford College apartment just above us. He was a white Englishman, totally disaffected, and a resident in the college only by dint of the spousal dole. His wife had the full-time job. She was a nice American woman, dead plain in her dealings with the world. She was also a first-rate British Victorianist and a loyal member of the English Department faculty. One afternoon during spring term as I was minding my own business—the new Jackson Five album playing, our hall door open to catch a breeze—the chap from upstairs stepped inside unannounced and uninvited. He stared quizzically around at our stuff, and out of the blue asked: "Houston, do you know there was a great deal of controversy about your coming on board?"

"What're you talking about, man? I don't know anything about controversy. By the way, did I miss your knocking on the door?"

"I mean, Houston, you know why you are here, right?"

I certainly knew why I was in that place called Yale. I was working unbelievably hard to make a career of it and not get caught napping on the job, and I said so.

"No, that's not what I mean," he wagged at me. "That's not what I mean. Everybody works hard here. I'm just trying to tell you that you are here because you are a Negro. You're a black man. You never would have gotten the job if you weren't a Negro."

"Oh, *that!*" I said.

Some years down the line, I learned this man had committed suicide. Perhaps his morbid obsession with affirmative action drove him mad. As much as I hate the fact of his painful death, I also deplore the fact that he was utterly convinced I needed to do nothing but be "Negro" to maintain my place at Yale. There are times when I fantasize I might have adopted the role of academic race hustler that came into vogue when traditionally all-white colleges and universities went in search of "color." My eyesight and energy level today (not to mention my income) would probably be considerably better. But that was not to be. I had to engage in serious intellectual inquiry on all matters germane to my participation in the academy—hence I felt it necessary to go in search of black studies.

Fortunately, New Haven during the late '60s, as I have already suggested, was a busy, complex, demanding, and hugely informative place for black life and learning. It was a fine time to be alive and well and black in New England. Complementing other New Haven constituencies were the black faculty at Yale, who represented the cream of a fairly exclusive crop, meaning, of course, that black Ph.D.s in such institutions were extremely rare in 1968. There was Ken Mills in philosophy and Roy Bryce-Laporte in sociology and anthropology, Arna Bontemps and Austin Clarke in English, John Clark in psychology, Carmen De Lavallade in drama, Richard Goldsby in biology, James Comer in psychiatry—and the visitors: Sylvia Boone, Paule Marshall, Geoffrey Holder, and others. It was high times for the black intellectual enterprise in the world of Yale and New Haven. I thus had many local sources and a number of friends across the nation to consult on the matter of black studies. From my various consults (some of them more hair-raising than others—like the assassination of John Huggins and Bunchy Carter at a black studies development meeting at UCLA)—I discovered there was already a large consensus on the basic requirements for black studies in the university:

• A program must be autonomous (i.e., independently black-owned and -operated, possessing the same departmental autonomy as traditional university disciplines).

• A *program* in black studies should represent a brief interval in the journey toward full departmental status. Hence, even at the program level, black studies must be endowed with significant fiscal resources (i.e., guaranteed, long-term apportionments from the university's operating budget). Imperative also is that the program have chief oversight of its own fiscal resources.

• Black studies must have access to all perquisites that mark departmental status in the university. Such perquisites include

authorized and budgeted new hires, fully resourced and cen-
tralized physical space and adequate staff to manage it, fellowship and scholarship support for graduate and undergraduate
students, and the right to manage the tenure and promotion
of faculty.

• Black studies must articulate—and set programmatically in
action—an agenda that expands the boundaries and definitions of "legitimate" academic work and knowledge to include
ongoing concern for the black majority, its life chances, and
the enhancement of its urban existence in America.

• An effective and empowered program must commence with a
graduate research arm and a "diasporic" component in place.
Thoughts of an Afro-American studies Ph.D., in other words,
must never be *afterthoughts*.

• An effective black studies program requires top-down, pro-
tected status—something akin to the ecological sanctions
surrounding endangered species. The translation of this protection clause would often result in black studies reporting to
the president or provost, and not to lesser deans.

Having learned and digested these rudimentary requirements,
I felt my knowledge and understanding of black studies was, at least,
adequate for committee purposes. I was bold enough, of course
(being young and blissfully naïve), to think I might even provide
some leadership on the committee (an early, egotistical foreshadow-
ing of my thought that I should be invited to the inaugural Faulkner
conference in Mississippi). Boldness is often the servant of absurdity.
I had not even been introduced to the principals in Yale's extensive
process of black studies formation, nor had I attended the symposium, nor was I networked in any way with anybody who truly
mattered in the planning process.

(It is important, as a twenty-first-century afterthought, however, to note that my hiring occurred during the winter of 1968, and
no black faculty member, staff, student, organization, committee,

or assembly ever graced my wife's or my life via telephone, letter, telegram, or other available means of communication. We were not welcomed to Yale, assisted upon our arrival, or even spoken to by any black faculty member or black Yale student whatsoever. One might ask, then, in a certain hard retrospective reading of events, if the black student and faculty insiders in Yale's black studies program were as exclusive an elite as, say, members of that secret cadre called Skull and Bones. How savvy were they, that is to say, in the matter of community as a prerequisite to radical change?)

I knew I needed allies. I needed "brothers" beside me in the process of achieving the leadership for which I dreamed I was destined. There could be no going it alone. So I telephoned the other black faculty on the black studies committee—Professor James Comer and Dean Paul Jones (a recent Yale graduate). I asked them to come to Branford College for a working lunch. We agreed we would meet on the afternoon before the committee's first session.

The three of us showed up wearing jackets and ties. We shook our collective heads in disdain at the paltry resources designated for black studies. We mused in common about why a "white man" (Professor Mintz) had been chosen to lead a black enterprise. We waxed eloquent on the needs of "our people" in urban America—especially those in the Hill and Dixwell black communities between which Yale was inexorably situated. Finally, on the fundamental and nonnegotiable *requirements* of black studies, no more unified band of brothers could be found than we three. I said: "We are agreed, then: We will *not* sign off on or endorse any plan that does not include *all* the requirements?" "That sounds right to me!" said Comer. Jones extended his palm, and said: "Right on!" I slapped his hand, feeling the unity.

I showed up sharp for the first full meeting of the committee the next day. I mean, I was pressed, from my stocking-cap-disciplined hair to the tips of my newly glossed Florsheim shoes. I winked at Comer and Jones before taking my seat at the stately conference table in one of those sumptuous, wainscoted rooms at Yale.

Professor Mintz showed up, decidedly *not* pressed. He wore a short-sleeved shirt, rumpled khakis, and casual shoes. What was most in evidence, though, was a cocky conviviality. Something on the order of: "Whose native enterprise this is, I think I know." He began the meeting, and ended it. He did not stop talking. He informed us of the long-range plan for black studies at Yale and how our black soon-to-be colleague, John Blassingame (whom I had known as an instructor at Howard University when I was an undergraduate), was the greatest young black historian known to man, doing ground-breaking work before taking up his post in Yale's black studies program. He continued, saying that his own colleague, Roy Bryce-Laporte, was going to be an enormous boon to the program; he was an amazing scholar in formation. He went on, and on, and on, until it seemed suddenly—as on a San Francisco morning the fog lifts—he became aware that there were others at the table. "Any questions?" he asked.

I was on my feet faster than Muhammad Ali on Sonny Liston's jaw: *"Having read the plans and consulted with 'the people,' we blacks on this committee do not feel the current plan meets the minimum national consensus and requirements for a first-rate black studies program. We demand, therefore, independence, tenured faculty, a proper research and community component. We also demand a budget commensurate with program goals and adequate space in which to house it. Finally, I think I speak for us all when I say we demand, at Yale, a program sufficient to address the black urban needs of 'the people' of New Haven and of the United States as a whole."*

It all ran out in a single breath. Mintz was stunned, and appeared, quite frankly, enraged. His eyes flashed confusion. Clearly, this was not what he had anticipated. A twenty-five-year-old skeleton of a Negro, who had been in New Haven for less than a year, was confronting his eminence and wisdom and making demands?

I do not remember precisely what happened next. I know Professor Mintz had the presence of mind to say something—angrily and imploringly—to my "brothers," Comer and Jones. They had my back, right? Our watchword was "Unity!" But I had seriously miscalculated. Comer and Jones looked him "straight in de eye" (as that line from *Porgy and Bess* would have it) and coolly announced: *"The opinions expressed by that breathless Negro do not represent our sentiments or assessment of the great potential represented by the Yale black studies plan. Sid, you know we are on board. We have been on board from the start. You definitely have us headed in the right direction!"* (This is my paraphrase of the brotherly response as I recall it these many years down the line.)

It was my turn to be flustered. Confused. Completely taken aback. Here I was—as Ellison's *Invisible Man* states—"Sambo, out on a lambo!" I was indisputably bowling alone. Professor Mintz declared: "The meeting is adjourned!"

When I got back to Branford College after the meeting (a fifteen-minute walk, at most), there was a note on my apartment door: "Please come and see me immediately. Signed: T. E., Dean of Branford College." I made my way downstairs and across the courtyard, to the office of "T. E." He was no older than I. He had recently graduated from Yale. He seemed to be serving as an Ivy League apparatchik while looking for a way to convert undergraduate capital accrued as an ice-hockey team roustabout and philosophy major into meaningful salaried employment in Manhattan. He opened the office door at my knock and with a fiendishly amused grin asked, "What did you *do* to Sid Mintz?" (There it was again . . . a vague question out of the white-blue at Yale. Not unlike: "You know why you are here, right?") I suppose I might have been expected to roll my eyes wildly like those monstrous black caricatures of early American silent films with a caption underneath reading: "O Lawdy, Mr. T. E., has I done something to make Mr. Sid mad?" In fact, I told T. E. I didn't know what he was talking about. And he said: "Sid called a few minutes ago. He was furious! He asked if you were . . . well . . . he asked if you were crazy."

"Hold up, T. E., just hold up," I said. "He asked you *what?* If I was *crazy?*"

"He asked if we had experienced any problems with you as a fellow of Branford College. He wanted to know if we noticed any unusual behavior. He suggested we might, perhaps, be vigilant before you hurt someone. Shit, Houston, he wanted to know if you were crazy."

Crazy? I had stood up in a meeting and passionately expressed what seemed a local and national consensus about the organization, goals, and protocols of black studies. *Crazy?* My declarations apparently qualified as madness. I had spoken, yes, breathlessly, in terms of "the people." But . . . *crazy?*

Maybe the thought crossed Sid's mind because I had tried seriously (truth to tell) to sound like a Black Panther when, in actuality, I was only a black sprite of a UCLA Ph.D. The venerable, white, ac-

ademic all-star Professor Maynard Mack had recruited me to Yale.
I was hired as a British Victorianist for the English Department. What
was I doing at Sid's black studies table? A fair enough question, given
what I have already confessed about my limited experience. Still, the
judgment *crazy* seemed harsh. It was, however, my first job in the
traditionally all-white academy. I didn't yet have a handle on what
from a black academic is considered crazy by white committee chairs,
and most white others on the job. All these matters swirled as T. E.
droned on about "collegiality" and other such words he had learned
as an undergraduate at Yale. The entire episode gives me the willies
even thirty years later. White planners, black "unity," academic in-
tegrity, and, most important, the commitment of black men and
the white academy to the well-being of the black majority—these
challenging, volatile, problematic matters all came out in that single
incident.

My first acquaintance with black studies was thus—as one might
say at Yale—a proleptic metonym. In my maternal grandfather's
church in Louisville, Kentucky, it would be called a "sign and a won-
derment," like lightning bolts from God suggesting that a radical,
liberatory black imagination can get you into a heap of trouble in
any white American institution.

A carefully conceived, fully consultative, black-majority-oriented,
urban-invested, and adequately financed black studies project is ter-
rifying to the American academy. If overseen and independently
managed by black men and women who cannot be bought, bossed,
or bullied, such a project is doubly troubling to white academics. In
a word: it's crazy.

Of course, my wife and I were not kicked out of Branford College. However, no one at Yale or in New Haven seemed remotely
able to foresee that craziness itself was about to come to town-
and-gown in the spring of 1970. Craziness—in the form of people
of radical politics of all stripes—arrived at Yale/New Haven's construction site of black studies in 1970. Black Panthers, Jean Genet,
Abbie Hoffman, Benjamin Spock, and approximately fifteen thousand other revolutionary participants assembled on the town com-
mons for a May Day gathering. They were intent on a new view
of Yale, a transformation of New Haven into a realistic example of

a model city, and the transmogrification of the United States into a land that would condemn imperialism, give the "Negro" a fair shake, and redistribute the world's wealth. The arrival of this wave of "craziness" might be considered the Second American Revolution, meant to save the world and empower the people.

So everyone must know this: the project of black studies at Yale did not come into being as a result of a Ford Foundation sponsorship, or a Yale black undergraduate symposium, or the complicit eagerness of people like Comer and Jones to lend black faculty support to undergraduates and their man Sid. No—men and women who were black, urban, streetwise, and just a little bit crazy instituted black studies at Yale, effectively and powerfully. The founding of black studies at Yale was a combination of hyper-American black urban realism and the nonconformism of the best and brightest of Yale's rosters. There was, in fact, something in that 1970 May Day's revolutionary moment that seemed closely akin to the New England genealogy of men like Thoreau and Emerson. Such New Englanders chose race and class treachery on behalf of a black, enslaved majority in the United States. I would earnestly suggest that black studies at Yale found its genuine inaugural breath as a direct result of that crazy May Day convergence of uncowardly men and women from all sectors of America, willing to go to jail for justice, eager to hear freedom ring from sea to shining sea. Yes, there was a neonate, as it were, in the birthing room at Yale/New Haven, but the slap on the bottom needed to set the baby breathing was May Day 1970. There were exploding tear-gas canisters in downtown New Haven, a Yale chaplain who was not afraid to take religion into the fray, and everywhere there was the cry: *The ultimate solution is black revolution!*

Why, then, does one white Yale emeritus professor now remember the first cry of Yale black studies as follows: "In an age of unruly protests, they [black undergraduates campaigning for an end to the lies of the Yale curriculum and the banality of white extracurricular excess] used polite diplomacy, reason and research." And how can one former black undergraduate "revolutionary" recall those heady, revolutionary times in the following words: "We knew that our best weapon was intellect. We made a strong rational argument that stood on its merits."

How soon we do forget, rewrite history, throw up barricades against craziness! Maybe Sid Mintz was an "intuitive" when he labeled me crazy. Perhaps that first full assembly of the black studies planning committee was all a thing of precognition. Maybe he foresaw that, by the twenty-first century, everyone would remember reason, intellect, cocky conviviality, diplomacy, and "can't we all just get along" banality as the big winners in the establishment of black studies at Yale.

The truth? Yale's black studies program missed the boat and the beat of the times altogether and its potential to intervene in the ever-deteriorating conditions of black urban America—just around the corner, on both sides of the university. And yet there was one at Yale who did step forward and embrace the craziness. "I am skeptical," said President Kingman Brewster, Jr., "of the ability of the black revolutionaries to achieve a fair trial anywhere in the United States." Two observations seem in order.

First, I believe Yale became a decidedly urban university in that revolutionary moment of black studies' solidification that was May Day 1970. If Kingman Brewster had been a Black Panther (as crazy as it sounds) and in charge of black studies at Yale, then the whole of the university and, arguably, New Haven itself, would be far better, safer, financially backed urban venues and places of knowledge formation than they are today. Alas, craziness and Kingman Brewster did not triumph. Within the past two decades, drugs, alcohol, murder, and a decidedly deindustrialized American variety of racial segregation, have come *from* Yale and New Haven as daily warrants of the failure of a potentially powerful program initiative. Downtown has been boutiqued in New Haven, but the black majority is worse off than ever.

Observation number two: In that moment of possibility that was black studies formation at Yale, many black academics—privileged enough to be on board in New England—made a career shift to the study of the lives and work of men and women of color. I was among the happy few. As a black intellectual constituency, we relinquished all faith in the traditional triumphalism of white Western "civilizing missions." Simply stated, we came to see that the West's wealth, leisure, art, culture, and "reason" (the antonym of "craziness") were built upon the stolen land and stolen labor of American chattel slavery. Who among us could be for reason as it manifested itself in the murder and mayhem of the transatlantic slave trade and its diasporic aftermath?

I think our shift in intellectual focus—we, the May Day people—has during the past three decades affected the American academy in profound ways. At the very least, a traditionally all-white American academy has been compelled to see—let us not be too grandiose—difference as a legitimate ground for serious intellectual investigation and challenging scholarly work. Such difference was at one time labeled crazy.

But these ruminations on black studies are just a story. They are memoir. They are, in a sense, simply other family musings. They are self-referential and subject to historical and empirical correction. I have come to think that memory is an involuntary muscle—it cannot help presenting its bearer in a more complimentary light than he deserves.

And yet, these many seasons past Yale/New Haven, I am willing to wager that if one randomly asked a black man or woman on the American street where one might find a black studies program actively enhancing his life chances, he or she would respond: "I don't know where that might be." There are many miles to go before we reach Mount Zion, though we have indeed made giant steps. Black studies is as real as rain—and as enduringly influential among progressive academics in America as the earth itself. Nevertheless, we have to guard our black studies enterprise and personnel against the all-purpose, conservative, tricky charge of *craziness* as we strive to act on behalf of the black American majority. I think there is a reason my memories of first acquaintance with black studies at Yale include a very bleak winter—that "true north" season in New Haven when precious little goodwill blooms.

The Poetry of Impulse

BLACK WORDS ON SOUTHERN GREEN

One of my most vivid memories from my late twenties is the stunning greenness of the springtime South. New England winters are colorless. They are also long—dropping snow and ice that make it feel like Antarctica. During my wife's and my second year in New Haven, it had been so seriously wintry that I still recall an unusual May afternoon. On that day, the sun's brightness was a marvel, and I reasoned: "Surely I can sit in the Branford College courtyard and read. Spring is here!" I spread a blanket and sat down. I never opened the book. A wintry shock assaulted my bottom faster than a speeding bullet, tearing through the blanket and my corduroy slacks. The season had not changed. Only the quality and quantity of New Haven light had shifted. I detest winter's monochrome bleakness, despise its depressing early dark. I was soon to discover a striking alternative when on a frigid, overcast morning, my wife and I boarded a cramped Allegheny Airlines flight headed south. Two hours later, we descended narrow aircraft stairs into the lush green and riotous spring colors of

Charlottesville, Virginia. Added to my memories of vivid green are red azaleas, pink rhododendrons, and white dogwood. It was as though we had entered a different galaxy. We were in the green South.

But I should back up. We did truly understand—spring colors notwithstanding—that we were unequivocally in *the* South. Our high school and college years had witnessed nightly television images of snarling police dogs attacking neatly dressed civil rights protesters. Virginia was only seven hundred miles from the scene of Emmett Till's murder, an event with its open-coffin funeral that traumatized our black generation. Schwerner, Chaney, and Goodman had disappeared in the Mississippi South on June 21, 1964. The FBI discovered their mutilated bodies forty-four days later, entombed in an earthen dam. Moreover, Virginia itself shut down public school systems in order to prevent desegregation. Still . . . we were breathless with excitement when first we saw the paradisiacal green of Charlottesville. The University of Virginia made a job offer (including doubled salary, tenure, and much more) that I could not refuse. As we reached cruising altitude on our flight back to New Haven, I turned to my wife and said: "Well, honey, I guess we have a lot to think about." She responded: "What's to think about?" She had had it with both New Haven and winter. Secretly, we believed we had discovered a southern Shangri-la. For example, the entering class of 1974 (the year our residence began) would for the first time in the history of Mr. Jefferson's university enroll a significant number of women and blacks. Charlottesville was green, and progressive, we believed.

Ah, but *green* is a complicated matter, as I hope to make clear in the following reflections. Things began to fall apart fairly quickly in our first return to the South. Charlottesville's regional, local, and institutional racism came to the fore all too chillingly, almost trumping the bleak shock of cold on that sunny afternoon in New Haven. I shall reserve for another time a full account of the downhill slide. But I cannot leave the matter without rehearsing one family tale that haunts us to this day.

My wife determined that daycare was just the right option for our three-year-old son. With her usual efficiency, she secured references and telephoned various schools with cute names like Winnie's Hideaway. One director enthused: "Why, yes, we can use boys, and we certainly have vacancies for the kind of energetic little fellow you describe." When my wife arrived for her scheduled appointment the next day, however, the director answered the doorbell, blanched, and stumbled back upon her heels as though she had just seen Clytie's ghost (that gothic specter from Faulkner's *Absalom, Absalom!*). She stammered: "You . . . um . . . didn't tell me . . . we are pretty much full . . . and . . . " My wife cut her off mid-stammer, insisted upon going inside for her scheduled inspection tour, and knew our son had been racially rejected before he even had an inkling of what the South can do to body and soul. She left with her heart shredded and her anger boiling. It was truly an ugly moment. The progressive dream was not to become a reality, it seemed. Within a few months of the daycare fiasco and a train of southern insults I must save for another time, we were seriously pursuing alternative employment options. We headed north (after four years of duty completed) and back to winter. As we belted ourselves into our Allegheny Airlines seats, my wife turned from gazing out the window and said: "The South is crazy, like a beautiful but evil woman!"

It has taken many years to realize that what happened to us in Charlottesville was archetypal for the black American experience on New World home ground. We had been attracted to Charlottesville by its beautiful, temperate, and almost uncannily familiar landscape. I was, after all, born in Louisville, where "My Old Kentucky Home" floats melodiously over the green air of Churchill Downs during the Derby. My wife was reared in Washington, D.C., with its sultry southern summers, and was shipped off every July to her father's people in Ahoskie, North Carolina. All our senses, therefore, combined with the lush green of the landscape to seduce us into Charlottesville reverie and desire. Situated at the foothills of the Blue Ridge, with tolerably humid red/orange/yellow sunsets, we felt we were "home."

By dint of a *sui generis* black history that formed our childhood consciousness—a consciousness inspirited in our recent past by the black liberation struggles of May Day and black studies energies of the late 1960s and early 1970s—we just knew our essential being in the world was informed by, yes, transatlantic dread, but also a remarkable ancestral past.

We were of the southern vale so eloquently analyzed by Du Bois; its spaces and places and grotesque contraries were our green land of promise. It was where we wanted our son to be at peace, and to grow and mature in wisdom. Little did we realize the complexities of southern antinomies: magnificent black sorrow songs and brutal white spectacle lynchings; dignified black entrepreneurship against the grain and white convict-lease incarceration; and inspiringly resilient black idealism and white mutilation and burial of black bodies unpunished by the law.

Awe-inspiring natural beauty is but a metonym for the regional trap and southern incarceration of the abjected black body. Du Bois's prose is rapturous in its descriptions of the almost sublime landscape of southern zones through which he travels. But such descriptions are always held in counterpoint by depressing portrayals of black settlements marked by ramshackle churches and one-room dwellings housing black families of as many as twelve. "Without contraries," writes William Blake, the English poet and mystic, "is no progression." Blake's words are prophetic with respect to African American experience and expression of the South.

For one might surely claim that the South's most egregious violence has been directed at and has immemorially harmed black bodies in the Americas. Such outgoing violence constitutes one pole of the bipolarity suggested by *black*. The contrary to such immediate violence is a gospel of *agape* (spiritual love), formulated, preached, and lived revolutionarily by one of the greatest liberation movement orators of all time, Dr. Martin Luther King, Jr. Dr. King instituted—in large measure through poetic oratory and resounding words which aimed to make black America and the United States whole—an unstoppable social movement often summed up by reference to his famous "I Have a Dream" speech delivered at the Lincoln Memorial in Washington, D.C., in June of 1963. King's speech was a brilliant performance of antinomies! The movement he led and his oratory are undeniably commensurate with the declaration: "I don't hate the South."

At the national Mall in 1963, Dr. King moved from a white American "bad check" issued to black America to a contrasting, sublime vision of Georgia's red hills sacralized by the integrated play of black and white children bound by a national gospel of *agape*. In the good doctor's classic speech, an American national polity is allegorically projected as "free at last" of its ignominious past and present institutional racism. At least that is the desirous goal of Dr. King's evocative words. He wove beauty, violence, and utopian futures into a speech driven, preeminently, by desire. One way of summarizing this is to say that, if bitterness, hatred, and violence are reflexive behavioral and rhetorical responses to life behind an imprisoning Jim Crow vale, then lyrical, idealistic, meditative, visionary, and progressive iterations of a better life represent the better impulses and angels of the black American people.

I use the word *impulse* as an imperfect synonym for "desire" considered as aspiration, yearning, wish, longing. And I intend *desire* in the sense instituted by the French intellectual Jacques Laçan. In layperson's shorthand, I want to say that Laçan believed we achieve our identities through language. Language is but representation and always symbolic; what we perceive as our coherent and whole selves in the mirror are never, actually, who we say, or are linguistically labeled as, or can prove we *are*.

In a sense, language as the gateway of our identity is like a carnival hall of mirrors. There is, thus, always a gap, a lack, an unconquerable divide that the black writer Richard Wright captures in the title of one of his better known poems: "Between the World and Me."

When we fall into language (which Laçan defines as patriarchal, causing scholars like Gilles Deleuze, Felix Guatari, and Judith Butler to dissent from his thesis), we join the world. But we lose our whole(ness). We are always attempting, according to Laçan, to fill the "hole in the self" that is our identity formation. We do this through our desirous acquisition of things: perfect cars, outstanding boyfriends, trophy wives, more money. But we always fail at wholeness, because desire is insatiable. Du Bois desires a "better truer self." He desperately wishes to suture his being, as self, to the mirroring image held exclusively by "that other world," which does not know and does not want to know the power of a whole W. E. B. Du Bois. Black folk (in this Du Boisian doubling so eloquently detailed in *The Souls of Black Folk*) are always emblematic, I think, of a Lacanian prospect in which the only possible black American identity is a "me no-body knows"—a universe of discourse in which "nobody knows my name." Du Bois's "double consciousness," Richard Wright's "ethics of living Jim Crow," Ralph Ellison's "invisibility," and Toni Morrison's "dark" playground of *Playing in the Dark*—these are all signifiers of black American desire for a new American *wholeness*. Desire haunts the vale as enduringly as heavy humidity burdens North Carolina summers. *Impulse,* then, is in my definition of an insatiable, lyrical, antinomian longing for black wholeness; its work consists, at least in part, of extolling southern green.

I think black American expressive culture—especially given what might be called the Calibanistic relationship of diasporic Africans to Western language ("You taught me language," says Caliban in *The Tempest,* "and my profit on't / Is I know how to curse. / The red plague rid you / For learning me your language!")—is singular in the production of what I will call a *poetry of impulse.* "The South is like a beautiful but evil woman!" said my wife as we headed north. I think "evil" for her signals a fragmentation, a lack that leads to the impulsive search for wholeness and beauty—in short, to the expressive quest for a South one must never hate because it is ancestral ground filled with dread, because it is also the old country, as nourishing as bread. We left the Virginia South in 1974.

Fast forward thirty years!

It is 2004, and Professor Joanne V. Gabbin of James Madison University has asked me to keynote the second Furious Flower poetry conference. I choose as my title: "Black Words on Southern Green: The Poetry of Impulse." My first sighting relevant to my title is a scene from Ralph Ellison's *Invisible Man.* The protagonist of Ellison's novel is black and in the South. Seeking to understand mysteries of black/white southern relationships, he undergoes a dreamy scene of instruction. He is perplexed by a black woman who says to him: "I dearly loved my master, son. . . . He gave me several sons . . . and because I loved my sons I learned to love their father though I hated him too. . . . I loved him and give him the poison and he withered away like a frost-bit apple." Stunned and confused, the protagonist asks how she can love someone and, at the same time, be moved to obliterate him. The woman explains her master promised to free her and her sons from slavery before he died, but in his final illness he reneged. She poisoned him, she says, to prevent his illegitimate sons from tearing the white master/father "to pieces with they homemade knives." The protagonist sort of gets it, and sort of doesn't. He has earlier responded to the woman's story: "I too have become acquainted with *ambivalence*" (my italics). What, queries the black woman, is "ambivalence"? "Nothing," says Ellison's antihero, "a word that doesn't explain it." In reality, *ambivalence* does almost always mark the complex, poisonous, lyrically rebellious, condemnatory psychology of black south existence—and of a discrete form of black southern poetry. In a sense, it is precisely ambivalence that is the hallmark of the black American expressive cultural tradition. In my conference keynote, I turned, therefore, to a poetry that captures ambivalence—those intricate love/hate sentiments and poetic, psychologically desirous reaction formations encapsulated in the episode from *Invisible Man*. Of course, I designated such poetry: The Poetry of Impulse. One of the most prominent examples of such poetry is constituted by the form, settings, characters, and lyricism of Jean Toomer's famous Harlem Renaissance work titled *Cane*, published in 1923.

Cane is a beautifully complex, controversial, short, and infinitely compelling expressive collage that everyone with a love for literature should read. *Cane*'s plot is divided into three sections set in the South, the North, and returning again in the closing section to the South. The closing section is titled "Kabnis" after the name of its main character, Ralph Kabnis, a black northerner who comes south in search of black ancestral "root wisdom." Taking a teaching job at a backwater black school in the South, Kabnis commences his quest to learn and express the "truth" of what is earlier described in *Cane* as "strong [black] roots [that] sink down and spread under the river and disappear in blood-lines that waver south."

Kabnis is by turns enamored and terrified of what he discovers during his roots sojourn. We meet him at an anxious, insomniac moment in the shabby, rodent-infested quarters to which he has been assigned by the black school principal, Hanby. It is a moonlit night in Georgia during which poetry seems to arise from the warm earth and descend from a starry sky with a single refrain:

> White-man's land.
> Niggers, sing.
> Burn, bear black children
> Till poor rivers bring
> Rest, and sweet glory
> In Camp Ground.

Toomer's dark voice sings anxiously, struggling to distill the poetic essence of the South. Black children, who are shadow precursors to Emmett Till, are murdered. They are witness to the terrors of spectacle lynching. They feel in their pulses and sense in the cautious glances of their elders' store-porch conversations the unquestionable injustice of whites' possession of the land and supremacist power over black bodies.

Kabnis is mystical, overwrought, surging with geographical ambivalence. He is a poet. Sequestered in sagging, exposed, unfit quarters, he articulately flows like the "rivers" of which he speaks. His style and observations are the very essence of what I call the poetry of impulse. Here is his nocturne:

> If I could feel that I came to the South to face it. If I, the dream (not what is weak and afraid in me) could become the face of the south. How my lips would sing for it, my songs being the lips of the soul. Soul. Soul hell. There ain't no such thing. What in hell was that?

A sound breaks across the poet's flow. What is it? A barn rat—noisy precursor of Bigger Thomas's antagonist in the opening scene of Richard Wright's novel *Native Son* (1940)—breaks the poet's flow. Catching his breath, Kabnis continues:

> God Almighty, dear God, dear Jesus, do not torture me with beauty. Take it away. Give me an ugly world. Ha, ugly. Stinking like unwashed niggers. Dear Jesus, do not chain

me to myself and set these hills and valleys heaving with
folk-songs, so close to me that I cannot reach them
. . . Lynchers and business men . . . Oh, no . . . Curses and
adoration don't come from what is sane.

"Curses and adoration"—here is black expressive cultural precision. Kabnis's is a poetry that features adoration for what I have
defined in foregoing paragraphs as "southern green." At the same instant, he casts a conjurer's spell and curse on all houses of white
power and privilege that, for generations, have systematically made
"rats" in the homes of the black American majority as common as
The Cat in the Hat in secure, white, suburban households. Surely echoes
of earlier cited sentiments can be heard in *Cane*: "The red plague rid
you / For learning me your language!" Kabnis's intoxicated soliloo-
quies under the stars are adoringly impulsive because he feels that he
is one of the cursed—one could say Calibanistic—children of Ham.
But the southern poet in him is nearly overwhelmed by the sacred,
immemorial, sublime black geographies that seem to possess him.
He is brought to his knees by the black cultural epiphany about the
South's racial mentality—crazy, like a beautiful but evil woman.

Joining chorus in the poetry of impulse with Toomer is his famous
contemporary Langston Hughes. It is perhaps Toomer's Ralph Kabnis
who provides the most fitting model for Hughes's speaker in a stunning example of the type of poetry of impulse I am attempting to capture. The speaker of Hughes's poem titled "The South" rhapsodizes:

> The lazy, laughing South
> With blood on its mouth.
> The sunny-faced South,
> Beast-strong,
> Idiot-brained.
> The child-minded South
> Scratching in the dead fire's ashes
> For a Negro's bones.
> Cotton and the moon,
> Warmth, earth, warmth,
> The sky, the sun, the stars

The magnolia-scented South
Beautiful, like a woman,
Seductive as a dark-eyed whore,
Passionate, cruel,
Honey-lipped, syphilitic—
That is the South.
(*Collected Poems of Langston Hughes,* 26–27)

Seductiveness and cruelty, laughter and lynching, natural beauty and human treachery combine in Hughes's reverie to render landscape sensuously immediate and, at the same time, hauntingly threatening. This is both home and Jim Crow–imperiled no man's land. It is as sweet and recognizable as magnolia in May. But beneath silhouetted trees are charred black bones and the dark cooling ashes of white rituals of obliteration.

The sensory immediacy, affective duality, and lyrical response to assaults upon black body and spirit represented by Hughes are defining. They identify that special urge to "curses and adoration" (I almost said that *muse* of adoration and curses) that marks out a peculiarly ambivalent and geographically specific black poetry in the United States. This poetry originates from a historically situated black consciousness: a structure of feeling that is both lyrically adoring and literately resistant to the soul-destroying economics of New World slavery. It is a poetry of desire, multifaceted in its psychology and surprisingly and simultaneously rebellious and lyrical in its entry into language. Hughes's lyricist speaks for a black collective southern psychology when he says:

And I, who am black, would love her
But she spits in my face.
And I, who am black
Would give her many rare gifts
But she turns her back upon me.

The poetry of impulse represents black articulateness and lyricism in the very face of violence, catastrophe, rejection, and exploitation.

It transforms alienating territory into home ground through lyrical acts of consciousness.

I want as a final consideration briefly to reflect on Richard Wright's famous autobiography, *Black Boy*, and its southern engagement with the poetry of impulse. The impulsive resistance represented by Wright's acts of rebellion in *Black Boy* lends force to all currents of the narrative's flow. From the perspective of human action, such resistance is the stuff of folklore's most notorious "bad men" heroes, from Old English Beowulf to juke-and-jive Stackalee. Even at an improbably young age, Wright's autobiographical narrator is an outlaw with a portfolio—a black macho perpetrator of "thug life" on a black expressive cultural mission. Many critics have remarked on this harsh, outlaw strain of metaphysical rebellion. There is, however, in Wright's archetypically black southern narrative a less activist and strikingly nonaudacious undercurrent. It surfaces with the graceful majesty of dolphins breaking the waters of roughened seas. This quietly exquisite breach and flow is precisely the antonym of the curses, condemnation, and exposé that constitute the harsher strains of *Black Boy*. Wright's narrator stuns us, and like Toomer's Kabnis, transforms southern landscape with a poetic consciousness rich in the lyricism of place. He startlingly makes earth and sky, water and sun below the Mason-Dixon a sensuous black "home." He meditates as follows:

> The days and hours began to speak now with a clearer tongue. Each experience had a sharp meaning of its own.
> There was the breathlessly anxious fun of chasing and catching fireflies on drowsy summer nights.
> There was the drenching hospitality in the pervading smell of sweet magnolias.
> There was the aura of limitless freedom distilled from the rolling sweep of tall green grass swaying and glinting in the wind and sun.
> There was the feeling of impersonal plenty when I saw a boll of cotton whose cup had spilt over and straggled its white fleece toward earth.
> There was the slow, fresh, saliva-stimulating smell of cooking cotton seeds.

> There was the excitement of fishing in muddy country creeks with my
> grandpa on cloudy days.
> There was the relish of eating my first fried fish sandwich, nibbling at it
> slowly and hoping that I would never eat it up. (*Black Boy*, 52–53)

This is an extraordinary black southern engagement of the senses.
It is a sensuous report of everyday Delta life chanted by a narrator
whose body is plantation-bound by bleak expectations and lack. Yet,
under these most dread circumstances, it is capable of desirous and
sumptuous accountings of Delta earth, even an oxymoronic black
pleasure. Hence, even under crippling conditions of bodily abjection, the human spirit on impulse can (individually and collectively)
sing the "Lord's Song" in a strange land. We turn once more to Jean
Toomer's *Cane* and hear the following:

> The old woman lifted the well-lid, took hold the chain,
> and began drawing up the heavy bucket. As she did so, she
> sang. . . . Figures raised the windows and joined the old
> woman in song. Louisa and Tom, the whole street, sing-
> ing:

> Red nigger moon. Sinner!
> Blood-burning moon. Sinner
> Come out that fact'ry door.

A "blood-burning moon" is not only a sign of imminent death, but
in *Cane* it specifically prefigures the lynching of Tom (a black male
protagonist) in a white man's land. A black collective transforms the
moon's sumptuousness and mystery into a sorrow song.

Something on this order is precisely what marks the poetry of
impulse as it transfigures into an almost paradisiacal green landscape
of delicious discovery a land that burns black children, or lynches
fourteen-year-olds, or murders and entombs black and white civil
rights workers. The poetry of impulse shatters the communication
codes of Jim Crow that seem to mandate but two responses by black
America: silence, or a scream. It is desirous poetry that flows through
catastrophe like a current of distilled black southern consciousness.

I would claim that in its yearning transformations of abjection into wish, curses into adoration, it is a vibrantly expressive form of black American modernity. It perhaps parts company with the blues in its robust ability to do more than simply sustain a Du Boisian double consciousness and the instability of the blues. It strives toward wholeness in what might be thought of as a counterrepresentational poetics that puts Prospero to shame. Call it, if you will, a furious Lacanian flowering of black expression in the New World.

Modernity and the Transatlantic Rupture

SUGAR AND THE NEW SOUTH

A couple of years ago a friend of mine drew upon the modest artistic capital in my black poet's account to convince her colleagues to invite me to the Fifth International Meeting of Poets, in Coimbra, Portugal. The organizers of the meeting did not have unlimited funds, so I had to decide if going abroad on my own budget would be worth the whistle. I was mightily tempted from the outset because famous poets like Charles Bernstein and Seamus Heaney were slated to participate. But the money? Words my father had spoken many years earlier when I was considering a fellowship in Edinburgh returned to me: "Oh, no, son, we don't pass up opportunities like these!" I mentally bracketed the matter of money and accepted the invitation to Portugal. I had no idea at the time I would meet such captivating people, encounter such magical words and performances, and garner enough academic theoretical capital to be invited precisely one year later to an amazing Portuguese conference on modernisms.

The sounds, textures, and rhythms of the University of Coimbra (the oldest university in Portugal, dating to the fifteenth century) and Portuguese national culture became connected with modernism and southern poetry for me forever during the conference. In unexpected ways, the convergence of my two visits abroad (as my father would certainly have predicted) led to my fuller understanding of how the South became the fecundating *dirty black South* it is today. My enchantment with and acceptance by colleagues in Portugal—especially through our common conference engagements with "modernity"—gave me a welcome space for meditation on the global dimensions of a region begging to be more fully (and perhaps more impulsively) sung by scholars of our present generations. To "tell about the South," as one of Faulkner's well-known fictional moments has it, is to tell about a rupture—a transatlantic rupture of modernity, in which Portugal played no small part. I tell a version of that rupture's story and its southern implications here. Somehow it seems a necessary prelude (rather than merely a black self-storying) to an adequate comprehension of the South. It is unequivocally a necessary prelude to an informed reading of authors like William Faulkner and other "southern" writers. I therefore begin my tale in the present tense.

::

I have returned to Coimbra, a small Portuguese city two hours from Lisbon. I was here just a year ago for the Fifth International Meeting of Poets. My generous hosts afforded me the opportunity to perform the role of poet, reading on the last night of the festival, set in a wonderful theater in the student sector of the town. Now it is June 2005. Heat from irregular stone walkways seeps through the thin soles of my shoes. The Mondego River and its bright silver bridge shine as I remembered. Majestic Old World facades speak to ages far past. In Coimbra, slow time yields the colors of Mediterranean millennial glory.

Portugal has its own less-than-estimable history with respect to what in recent years we have come to call "the Other." (The origin of Other harks back to German *anders*: "anterior," "outside," "not oneself.") In the fourteenth century, Portugal was a seafaring nation devoted to God and gold (though not always in that order).

Its intrepid navigators made their way across vast oceans. Indeed it was the Portuguese prince Henry the Navigator who bankrolled and succeeded in putting his nation's ships past Cape Bojador, enabling navigation of the Guinea (West African) Coast. They pushed onward then to Cape Verde. Vast mercantile profits from these sea voyages included "captives" (African slaves), gold, and fortified lands and islands. There was also sugar.

Prince Henry's rationale for his country's oceanic profiteering was drawn significantly from his own notion of Other. His stated desire was to "extend the Holy Faith of Jesus Christ and bring it to all souls who wish to find salvation" (the chronicles or Zurara, quoted from *The Monks of War* by Desmond Seward). Presumably, for African souls, that salvation would take place somewhere other than mainland Portugal. Brazil perhaps? For there was scant evidence in Coimbra (or Lisbon for that matter) of a black Portuguese presence during my two visits.

The Universidade de Coimbra was founded as a kind of Portuguese Oxford, certainly the oldest seat of learning in the country. Regular group tours of the original university congregate outside impressive iron gates, while just next door stands the very modern home of the Faculty of Arts and Letters, complete with cafeteria and sturdy, bright, stadium-seat classrooms. The faculty is replete with well-read, cosmopolitan, and, in every conceivable way, modern scholars. They seem graciously capable of taking on any task with intellectual aplomb and hospitable good cheer. These scholars were perfect hosts for Modernismos (Modernisms), the two-day colloquium that brought me back to Coimbra. My assignment was to serve as final keynote speaker for the colloquium—an occasion meant to mark the conclusion of a collective research project conducted at the university's Center for Social Studies, titled "Memory, Violence, and Identity: New Comparative Perspectives on Modernism." The governing inquiry for the conference was: "What is, has been, and in future will be modernism?" And: "Why modernisms?" with an "s" signaling plurality. Participants included scholars from Holland and the United States, joining a sterling company of investigators and researchers from Portuguese universities and programs.

My very first impulse when invited was: "I have to tell about the South." I was not thinking in postmodern, political, or environmental terms of the grand divide of the world, which pictures a grossly underdeveloped "South" living in the overwhelming shadow of a resource-abundant "North." No, my response was directed precisely toward those U.S. states below the Mason-Dixon. For these counties and cities and suburbs and gated communities have radically transformed melodies and sentimentalisms like "The Old Folks at Home" into the rapid-fire lyrics and brilliant hooks and grooves of Dirty South hip hop, such as OutKast's "Player's Ball." The OutKast duo of André Benjamin (André 3000) and Antwan Patton (Big Boi) have devised a gritty language poetry that reflects, in every way, the neo-cosmopolitanism of southern U.S. capitals like Columbia, Baton Rouge, Nashville, and Atlanta. In fact, the academic journal *American Literature* is currently planning a special issue titled "The Global South." Having perused the prospectus for the issue, I realize more pointedly than ever that the American South is a booming, modern demographic, transforming itself steadily into headquarters for multinationals, with skyrocketing prices on ocean-front condos and mountain getaways, attracting Yankee expats by the scores of thousands. The South is also, of course, confronting the dark dilemmas of globalization, such as the vexed Mexican and Central American immigration, a deeply problematic new religious evangelism in tandem with old-time Dixie zeal for capital punishment, and an expanding private prison industrial complex. And of course there is the ever-thorny, nonbiodegradable, doggedly irresolvable issue of race. In U.S. vocabularies, to speak of "the race problem" is to call up precisely a single geographical region: *the South*. So, my goal for the Modernisms colloquium was to put together the geographies of Portugal and Birmingham, the salvationist goals of the good Prince Henry, and the so-called Mediterranean Accord (which I shall define shortly) with the rich deltas, productive rice paddies, billowing fields of snow-white cotton, and razor-sharp cane below the Mason-Dixon.

But how could I piece it all together to deliver a significant, southern talk in Coimbra?

As fate would have it, one of the university's doctoral candidates, Paula Mesquita, was delivering a paper on the first day of the colloquium, titled "Playing the Part in the War Theater: Gender as a

Battlefield in Cather and Faulkner." So the "s" on Modernisms was, assuredly, inclusive of Faulkner. The South was already in place in Coimbra. As it happened, Mesquita had been at the Yoknapatawpha conference in Oxford, Mississippi, when I presented the opening address in 2002. Her work is marvelously original, and we had a fine brief conversation about two southern writers who are very much in favor abroad: William Faulkner and Richard Wright. The South is certainly rising again in European literary and cultural studies and for, I think, *global* reasons.

Given the transnational cast of the colloquium, there seemed no better way to frame a discussion of modernism's rupture and the present-day U.S. South than in terms of the black diaspora. To do so is to call to mind transatlantic currents that have in recent years included popular music, films, and other expressions evocative of the history of blackness in motion. I commenced my presentation with a video montage (engineered by my colleague Professor Heather Russell Andrade of Florida International University) composed of scenes from the films *Amistad*, *Rosewood*, *Sankofa*, and *Life and Debt* (a brilliant documentary of modern Jamaican economics). The moving images were set to the sounds of Robert Nesta (Bob) Marley's "Redemption Song."

Quoting from Timothy White's *Catch a Fire: The Life of Bob Marley*, the Web site www.bobmarley.com notes that "Redemption Song" is

> a plaintive, almost Dylanesque acoustic spiritual song, devoid of any trace of reggae. When [Marley] sang it, he wore the expression of a playful child, but his voice bore the authority of a Biblical patriarch. . . . [It] is like a final statement in a career, a summation of all the themes and thought that had created it.

The lyrics of Bob Marley's production and prophecy read as follows:

> Old pirates yes they rob I
> Sold I to the merchant ships
> Minutes after they took I from the
> Bottom less pit
> But my hand was made strong

By the hand of the almighty
We forward in this generation triumphantly
All I ever had is songs of freedom
Won't you help to sing these songs of freedom
Cause all I ever had redemption songs, redemption songs

Emancipate yourselves from mental slavery
None but ourselves can free our minds
Have no fear for atomic energy
Cause none of them can stop the time
How long shall they kill our prophets
While we stand aside and look
Some say it's just a part of it
We've got to fulfill the book

Won't you help to sing, these songs of freedom
Cause all I ever had, redemption songs, redemption songs,
redemption songs

Won't you help to sing, these songs of freedom
Cause all I ever had, redemption songs
All I ever had, redemption songs
These songs of freedom, songs of freedom.

So, on a brightly sweltering day in Portugal, I commenced my keynote journey into a specific black modernism that still seeks its redemption, especially in the contemporary South. What better place to begin than with Marley's very words?

⠿

"Old pirates yes they rob I / Sold I to the merchant ships." Here we catch Marley in resilient recall, proclaiming the flowering of generations and soliciting us to join in "songs of freedom." Still, the images and emotions behind the music literally ache. The background is all fire and mutilation, dread immersions, sunstroke, backbreaking labor in blistering fields of cane. We infer a pride of legacy, but know it rides on restless seas where African bodies perished.

In his classic *The Souls of Black Folk*, W. E. B. Du Bois spoke of "the sorrow songs." In those old Negro spirituals, we are confined to memory and mourning, half-forgotten intonations of native languages raised collectively as shields against suicidal despair. To say, to sing, to line out black loss as sorrow songs, said Du Bois, is a halfway house of redemption. But the ineluctable, material facts of redemptively belated song remains. Which is the fact: *pirates yes they rob I / Sold I to the merchant ships.* Hence we imagine and cast ourselves back—two centuries in advance of Marley and Du Bois—and we can hear the cosmopolitan voice of one African autobiographer in medias res:

> The first object which saluted my eyes when I arrived on the coast, was the sea, and a slave ship, which was then riding at anchor, and waiting for its cargo. These filled me with astonishment, which was soon converted into terror, when I was carried on board. I was immediately handled, and tossed up to see if I were sound, by some of the crew; and I was now persuaded that I had gotten into a world of bad spirits, and that they were going to kill me. Their complexions, too, differing so much from ours, their long hair, and the language they spoke (which was very different from any I had ever heard), united to confirm me in this belief. Indeed, such were the horrors of my views and fears at the moment, that, if ten thousand worlds had been my own, I would have freely parted with them all to have exchanged my condition with that of the meanest slave in my own country. When I looked round the ship too, and saw a large furnace of copper boiling, and a multitude of black people of every description chained together, every one of their countenances expressing dejection and sorrow, I no longer doubted my fate; and, quite overpowered with horror and anguish, I fell motionless on the deck and fainted.

This is the account of Olaudah Equiano, recalling the horror of his preteen delivery to the coastal entrepôt of African enslavement. Equiano was but one of the more than *twelve million* Africans who in the course of four centuries fell victim to the almost unimaginably expansive, mercantilist, economic, religious, sociopolitical, and cultural network of the transatlantic slave trade.

When Olaudah Equiano (whose authenticity as an autobiographer of the trade is now under scholarly suspicion) and his sister were plucked from their family compound, it was not in the first instance by European "pirates." Rather, they were kidnapped by fellow Africans. "One day," says Equiano, "when all our people were gone out to their work as usual, and only I and my dear sister were left to mind the house, two men and a woman got over our walls, and in a moment seized us both, and without giving us time to cry out, or make resistance, they stopped our mouths, and ran off with us into the nearest wood." Months later, having changed African hands of transport and African masters of his labor many times, and having been forever separated from his family, Equiano arrives at the abject moment at the entrepôt already described.

The slave trade's network of multinational migration, kidnapping, and piracy extended inland from the African littoral and expanded outward through the Atlantic basin. The trade marked the intersection of African textiles, sugar island rum, European firearms, English swords, Gold Coast cowrie shells, and countless millions in Liverpool pounds sterling.

Of course, slavery's coextensiveness with bipedal human existence is indeed beyond doubt. The Web site for *New Internationalist* (a cooperative organization and magazine dedicated to reporting on issues of global poverty and inequality) tells us:

> Slavery began with civilization. For hunter-gatherers slaves would have been an unaffordable luxury—there wouldn't have been enough food to go round. With the growth of cultivation, those defeated in warfare could be taken as slaves. Western slavery goes back 10,000 years to Mesopotamia, today's Iraq, where a male slave was worth an orchard of date palms. Female slaves were called on for sexual services, gaining freedom only when their masters died. (www.newint.org)

But the modern economics of the transatlantic slave trade cannot be traced back through humanitarian pastoral apologetics for B.C.

agriculturalists, Roman senators, or, in the Equiano instance, African domestic slavers putting into bondage prisoners of tribal war. Rather than a lineal descendant, or heir, to slavery's antiquity, the transatlantic slave trade represents and enacts precisely a rupture with all slavery known before. In its raw brutality and global exchange, it literally and economically institutes the modern world. Its principal shifts toward modernity are as profoundly economic, psychological, legal, and political as they are technological and religious. These are the hard facts of the *longue durée* of what in our academic era we so nicely call "early modernism."

Global trade is as venerable as Mesopotamian agriculture and Homeric epic. However, the specific commerce of the transatlantic trade marks its networks, apparatus, justifications, motives, and goals as both commercially unique and ethically appalling. And in terse and fantastical shorthand, its eruptive difference is all about *sugar*.

The scene is a public thoroughfare in eighteenth-century London. King George and William Pitt the Elder observe the passersby. The king, witnessing a gold-leaved, elaborately filigreed coach of noble proportions, surrounded by servants, drawn by a choir of horses of the finest breed, demands of Pitt: "How came that fellow by his fortune?" To which Pitt replies: "Sugar, your majesty." The king's stunned response is: "Sugar? All that, sugar, Pitt!?" All that, sugar, indeed.

The adoption of systems of belief in tandem with crop selection, profitability, and modes of sugar production have collectively been labeled the Mediterranean Accord. In sugar production, profit was contingent upon legions of coerced labor. Coerced labor is an economics of theft, a sweet piracy. The large-scale, profitable utilization of coerced labor yielded the plantation as venue, and gang labor as mode of production. By the early seventeenth century, the plantation economics of sugar reached—in the first hugely profitable instance—Bengal and then moved outward to the sugar islands of the Antilles.

Here the material ethics of early modernity come into play. Church and state become complicit endorsers of the economics of the sugar trade: finding the indigenous populations of the so-called New World—the Indians—unsuited and unsuitable for coerced labor, Father Las Casas declares that the Native American population should be included among the "people of God." Where then should colonists seek that massive abundance of labor required for sugar production? Historian Peter Wood writes:

> The alternative of African labor was a plausible one at the outset. It appeared natural to colonizers from the West Indies and intriguing to those from western Europe, and it afforded certain advantages to both. Since Africans came from a distance, their exploitation did not present the serious diplomatic and strategic questions posed by Indian labor, yet their Caribbean sources were closer and their transportation costs lower than those of white workers. Unlike white servants, Negroes could be held for unlimited terms, and there was no means by which word of harsh or arbitrary treatment could reach their homelands or affect the further flow of slaves. (*Slavery Reader*, 228)

The historian Richard Dunn (in his classic *Sugar and Slaves*) captures with brilliant archival research the "wild," "frontier," "buccaneering," and "rapacious" conditions, illegalities, and protocols of global sugar: "it necessitated colonization. It yielded sumptuous profits and vast fortunes. It was unique in its demands—vast numbers of workers were needed all year long and through all seasons. Sugar plantations led, in turn, to the colonized production of tobacco, rice, indigo, and coffee."

In Portugal, bishops kept slaves and sanctioned slavery. In Rome, one pope was seen just outside the city on a summer's day "redistributing" the wealth of God—doling out, that is to say, a hundred African slaves recently bestowed upon him as a gift. In Spain, queens found their Indian New World "subjects" *dear*, while they regarded black Africans as heathens better served by "Christian enslavement." In England and its American colonies, Anglicans and Quakers, signers of the Declaration of Independence, and preachers by the boatload gave thanks to the Lord that the slave trade had brought "heathen souls" to their American chastening (while, of course, prodigiously boosting their savings accounts). Fortunes were made. Slave traders and bankers, silent partners and nobles, religious folk and adventurers alike were kin in the wild deportation of black bodies across a watery Middle Passage of bones and carnage, into forced labor. "O' voyage through death to life upon these shores!"

The point to be emphasized is that the transatlantic trade shifted national ideologies, populations, modes of production, definitions of race, and resistance in irreversible ways. And what is modernism but irreversibility? Humans ceased being an end in themselves and became a commodified *means* . . . a means, in fact and law, to greater means and fortunes. And Africans—the continental middlemen, such as the kidnappers of Equiano and his sister—were indispensable operators in the logics of the trade.

All were consumed with saving and spending—and the fungibility (that conversion of one thing into another) that made people into money. Fungibility is at the heart of modernism. The scholar Ian Baucom points out in *Specters of the Atlantic* that such an effective transvaluation, enabling actual human beings to become units of insurable worth, to be traded in a global system of credit and bills of obligation, represented, finally, the full effect of the Mediterranean Accord.

Following Baucom's lead, we can revisit the historical incident of the slave ship *Zong*, out of Liverpool. The ship was financed by the most portentous of the city's elite. It sailed into Kingston, Jamaica, harbor with a cargo of 132 captive, African bodies. Once there, however, the captain determined his "cargo" would not bring the price expected. The "cargo" was unfit. It would not add to the savings of all involved in the *Zong*'s global enterprise. The ship thus turned back to sea—and the crew one by one weighed down, tossed overboard, and drowned the ship's entire "cargo." The owners and backers of the *Zong* took the matter of their "insured loss" to English courts and were awarded in excess of £15,000 insurance compensation for the lost "cargo."

Such are the economics of the trade.

In time, owners of the *Zong* were instrumental in the erection of a new Exchange Building in Liverpool. What unique sign should mark the topmost bas-relief of this Liverpool monument to commerce? Why, of course, nothing could be more fitting than to circle the crown of the building with sculpted heads of "Guinea Negroes."

Are songs capable of helping to redeem such global piracy?

Can voyages through death ever be redeemed in the absence of a paradigm shift at least as global and monumental as the one that brought about the transatlantic slave trade?

What were the consequences of the trade in the United States? And what does this history have to do with a new millennial view of the American South?

First, the plantation economy was a disaster for biodiversity. No long explanation is in order here. Faulkner describes with more eloquence than any other writer of southern record the devastation wrought to everything "native" by stolen labor (those "wild niggers," in Faulkner's words) in "Sutpen's Hundred." Flora, fauna, valleys, hills, rivers (even the mighty Mississippi) utterly altered, exhausted, destroyed, flattened, razed by the necessities of converting a native natural landscape into an agricultural profit center.

By the time the first Reconstruction had run its brief course, prison camps and convict-lease labor, tenant farming and sharecropping, in conjunction with a general culture of white violence toward blacks, made agriculture in the South virtually synonymous with incarceration. And today, the South is home to the largest expanse of the private prison industrial complex in the United States. Prisons today are an archipelago of cheap labor—from incarcerated black and brown bodies acting as "customer service representatives" for global corporations, to black and brown women manufacturing blue jeans for well-known brands—where the average wage is under $2.00 a day. Moreover each prisoner is an economic unit, bringing in profit to corporations like Corrections Corporation of America and Wackenhut of millions of dollars a year for warehousing putatively "criminal" bodies. The Mediterranean Accord has morphed in the South from stolen to incarcerated labor. Each week, the private prison industrial complex reaps enormous (global) profit by locking down the undesirable Other, exploiting their bodies and labor. The complex is a vicious trace of modernism's first global rupture, and it can only be understood in historical terms. W. E. B. Du Bois said, "As goes the South, so goes the nation." The present-day reality in states below Mason-Dixon suggests the need for a new southern studies, focused precisely on the South. Three phenomena in particular underscore this urgent need: big-box stores' industrial dominance of local economies, immigration, and the rapid demographic expansion from Virginia to Florida, North Carolina to Mississippi.

Wal-Mart, founded by Sam Walton in the South (Arkansas) in 1962—with its exploitative, anti-union, politically conservative, and monumentally global outlook and practices—is the most egregious example of globalization's devastating impact on less-than-affluent communities. In Florida, Alabama, Georgia, South Carolina, North Carolina, Virginia, Mississippi, and of course, Arkansas, Wal-Mart operates (according to its own Web site) eight hundred supercenters and discount stores. It is the largest grocery chain in the United States, and its sales revenue for 2005 was $316 billion. While calling its low-wage employees "associates," the multinational Wal-Mart works more aggressively at anti-unionization and avoidance of benefits and adequate health care to its employees than its rivals such as Kroger and Costco. Though Wal-Mart's corporate propaganda depicts the company as the very heaven and haven of the doublewide oppressed, the corporation represents nothing but big-box economics. Its economies of scale and value lead to mind-numbing statistics like its $344 billion 2006 revenues and the millions worldwide who are dependent upon its meager wages and dubious largesse.

Recently, Wal-Mart corporate officials have been under legislative, community activist, union, and cinematic siege. In January 2006, the state of Maryland passed a bill requiring all corporations with more than 10,000 employees in the state to spend at least 8 percent of their payrolls on employee benefits, or pay into a state fund for the uninsured. Wal-Mart, with about 17,000 employees in Maryland, was the only known company to not meet this requirement before the bill was passed. Robert Greenwald's film *Wal-Mart: The High Cost of Low Price* is a sometimes tendentiously polemical—but intriguingly informative—documentary filled with interviews with Wal-Mart employees, who detail what they consider their gross exploitation by the chain. One practice of the corporation that has come under censure is called the "lock-in." During a lock-in, night managers lock the employees in the building overnight, supposedly to prevent theft. As of 2004, this practice was in effect at approximately 10 percent of Wal-Marts in the U.S. The aggregate of community response, employee description, and general human opinion seems to be that Wal-Marts in their general and their southern manifestations are retail juggernauts that might have done more than simply frighten Olaudah Equiano into a faint. It is likely that he would have been compelled to work himself to death at low wages, with no benefits, and under the shock of the sudden and unexpected nocturnal lock-in of a not-so-benevolent manager (master?). The transatlantic trade and new retail dynamics of the globalizing economy of the present can, perhaps, find no better avatar than the U.S. imperialism and wage bondage of Wal-Mart. Nevertheless, the aforementioned Maryland legislation was overturned by a higher court. Yet, in practical terms of "savings," how does one tell a black single father, working two jobs just to pay the rent, to go to Nordstrom or Macy's for the kids' clothes? Economies of scale in combination with truly criminal neglect of the men, women, and children furthest down in America have all average consumers over a Wal-Mart barrel. Then there is the southern matter of immigration.

According to U.S. Census Bureau data, seven of the fourteen fastest growing states in America are in the South: Florida, Georgia, North Carolina, South Carolina, Tennessee, Texas, and Virginia. Florida, with a percentage increase of 2.3 percent, has displayed the most rapid growth. Of course, the population increase in southern states has included immigrants from Mexico and Central America. By Census Bureau accounting, the East South Central Region—which includes Alabama, Kentucky, Mississippi, and Tennessee—has seen a 3,800 percent growth in Mexican workers, adding 112,000 workers to the region's labor force. Coupled with an exponential increase in low-skill, low-wage jobs, population increases of legal and illegal immigrants of Hispanic descent will be a central feature of southern demographics for the foreseeable future.

Recent concern among U.S. lawmakers and the general non-Hispanic populace mirrors a traditional United States' pattern of labor supply and demand from the south to the north of the U.S./Mexican border. In flush times, employers are eager to have as large a pool of Mexican and Central American laborers as possible. When downturns in the economy occur, employers want to send all "foreigners" home. In 2006, in protests against deportation and a prospective call to declare illegal workers "felons," tens of thousands of Mexican and Central American workers boycotted their jobs, took to American city streets, and demonstrated unequivocally their ability to shut down major sectors of the economy. They also revealed the extraordinary magnitude of their contemporary, politically active presence in the U.S.

Clearly, in the U.S. South, industries such as restaurants, motels, construction, hospitals, agriculture, landscaping, domestic house-cleaning, and car washes could not thrive without a huge reserve of Mexican and Central American labor. In intriguing ways, therefore, the pull factors of United States' employment are creating a version of that rupture of traditional borders and that demand for masses of poorly compensated labor that marked an earlier transatlantic trade. In the U.S. South, squalid subsistence-living conditions are frequently the norm for Mexican and Central American farm workers; their labor and lives mirror in dark ways chattel slavery's worst deprivations of body and spirit. The present migration of scores of thousands of Mexican and Central American bodies across dangerous zones of militarized surveillance and policing seems not unlike poor black tenant farmers or former slaves "without papers" trying to get someplace where they might have a chance of becoming modern, self-reliant, dignified, and decently paid laborers. Present-day "fugitive" immigrants make so many U.S. South geographies archetypically American.

So, for scholars busy with definitions of modernism and the dynamics of "nation," "immigration," and "location of culture," an at-hand laboratory is just a domestic plane ride away. Faulkner and Du Bois knew the South would always be the bellwether and index of Americanism in the global imagination. A meditation on "rupture," "globalization," "modernism," and the South does well to bear in mind the following observation from one of the essays that will mark the *American Literature* special issue titled "The Global South":

> [There is a pressing] need to think of southernness and southern geography as at best provisional, relational, as spaces that shift with various border crossings and that

are all the stronger for these processes. This also means
that we need to reorient southern studies from an "us vs.
them, blue vs. gray" axis to think the South more broadly,
allowing us to theorize the South's status as a hinge point
between the Americas. Think zones, not borders. (Tara
McPherson, "On Wal-Mart and Southern Studies")

Perhaps a reoriented southern studies might be listed under the
heading "redemption songs." For one of the most popular subgenres
of music currently heard around the world is called nothing other
than Dirty South. It is a type of hip hop featuring an astonishing mé-
lange of throbbing bass, gritty vocal stylings, vintage synth sounds,
black gospel intonations, blues harmonica riffs, and southern-fried
electric guitar leads, marketed through rapid-fire mass production
and eye- and ear-grabbing advertising. If one has not caught on to
OutKast, Goodie Mob, Master P, Mystikal, Nelly, Missy Elliott, Lil
Jon, Luther Campbell, Timbaland, T. I., and others of the emergent
"Durrty" South genre, then one is probably not ready fully to
engage in the project of reading and writing American, scholarly
redemption songs for a global future. Which is only to say, if you
have not listened in the past several years to the popular black songs
of the South (which are immeasurably different from those of
Mr. Disney), then you are probably missing a true picture of today's
modern America.

⁑

From Coimbra, it is on to Lisbon for me. The city is magical; its
magnificent boulevards are refulgent with the purple bloom of
jacaranda. On one swank Lisbon boulevard, a mega-global music
emporium throbs with OutKast's "The Way You Move." I think of
Faulkner.

Traveling with Faulkner

A Tale of Myth, Contemporaneity, and Southern Letters

"Faulkner and His Contemporaries" was the title of the 2002 Yoknapatawpha conference to which I was invited. It was necessary, therefore, not only to journey with the Bard of Rowan Oaks, but also to extend some consideration along the road to those of his contemporaries who influenced, shaped, or shared his creative projects. I quickly discovered that analyzing Faulkner's relationship to contemporaries is an expansive chore. His life covered more than sixty years and found him traveling abroad and cross-regionally in the United States, joining convivial associates in New York, New Orleans, Paris, and Los Angeles. To ask about his contemporaries, therefore, requires selectivity. If we look to his earlier contemporaries—or, better, influences—we discover a poetical Faulkner under the tutelage of his friend and first mentor, Phil Stone. At Stone's urging, Faulkner apprenticed his talent to Romantic and late Romantic poets such as Keats and Shelley, Aubrey Beardsley, and Algernon Swinburne. By the 1920s, however, he had taken up Conrad Aiken, A. E. Housman, James Joyce, T. S. Eliot, and other moderns. The moderns were to serve as formal guides for a good part of Faulkner's career.

But in the course of his travels and in the process of settling on his own principal theme, Sherwood Anderson played a significant, regionalist role for Faulkner. Author of the psychology and affective geographies of small-town America, Anderson enjoined Faulkner to concentrate his artistic labors on that "little patch of Mississippi" where he was born and reared. Anderson, thus, provided both an artistic model with his novel *Winesburg, Ohio* and a contemporary's usefully regionalist advice. He turned Faulkner's gaze and ambitions in a fruitful direction. He, in a sense, licensed the young man to be a southern writer—not simply another partisan in the lists of the moderns and Romantics.

Curiously, for a southern writer, Faulkner can scarcely be said to have acknowledged even a single Afro-American contemporary. The stores of black authors such as Jean Toomer, Langston Hughes, Richard Wright, and others remained an invisible marketplace to Faulkner, as they did to the literary-critical and cultural establishments that took their own sweet time recognizing even one of Faulkner's own artistic achievements. There can be little doubt, though, that when American literary-cultural establishments did "get into" Faulkner, they heralded him as indisputably modern and inescapably southern. I would like to suggest that T. S. Eliot's definition of the "truly new"—or in another phrasing, the truly "modern"—offers analytical possibilities for addressing the question of Faulkner and those who might be considered his contemporaries. Eliot suggests that the "really new" work of art is one that absorbs into itself and presents its own unique agon with a panoply of "existing monuments" that mark the creator's field of vision and endeavor as he commences his labor.

Now, I am fully aware that Eliot's notions are both conservative and set in a conservative frame of critical reference. But if we extrapolate from them—as we are free to do—then we can say that Faulkner's contemporaneity is as contingent upon his immersion in Greek and Latin classics as it is upon the Mississippi writer's modernist experimentation with stream-of-consciousness narration. The ground on which Faulkner reads as a traditionalist, therefore, might be thought of as a temporal plane spanning millennia, and yet as accessible and presently available as Rowan Oaks' library copy of *Ulysses*.

Holding across this temporal plane, moreover, is a formal constant drawn from our traditionalist reading of "contemporaries" and "contemporaneity." That formal constant is myth. Many of the English Romantics to whom Faulkner apprenticed himself were in substantial agreement with the prophetic William Blake, whose *Los* avers: "I must Create a System, or be enslav'd to another Man's." We think of Blake's masterful creation *The Vision of the Daughters of Albion* as one installment on this resolution. Blake's Romantic successors and their mythic Romantic creations include Shelley's *Prometheus Unbound*, Keats's *Endymion*, and Swinburne's *Atalanta in Calydon*. Faulkner's Romantic impulse yielded rich ore and has a distinct bearing on his own grandly illusioned and heroically soliloquizing figures, such as Thomas Sutpen, a mythic creation fully worthy of William Blake the prophet.

Glancing to London's literary circles of the 1920s, we recall another literary-historical moment in which myth is held to be coterminous with the best designs and legacies of the artist as social visionary. Again, we look to the criticism of T. S. Eliot. In an essay titled "*Ulysses*, Order, and Myth," Eliot writes:

> In using the myth [of Homer's *Odyssey*], in manipulating a continuous parallel between contemporaneity and antiquity, Mr. Joyce is pursuing a method which Others must pursue after him. . . . Instead of narrative method, we may now use the mythical method. . . . It is, I seriously believe, a step toward making the modern world possible for art. . . . And only those who have won their own discipline in secret and without aid, in a world which offers very little assistance to that end, can be of any use in furthering this advance.

Deploying "antiquity" to stage the modern was, of course, Eliot's game, as he demonstrated so persuasively in the richly allusive, mythical masterpiece *The Waste Land*. And Faulkner adopts from Joyce what Eliot notes as the "continuous parallel" and its possibilities for artistic modernism. Unlike Eliot, however, Faulkner and the past *tout court* were not twin souls, but rather feuding, baleful, inseparable alter egos in desolate counterpoint, savagely refusing to release one another to quiet certainty—or even simple rest.

We have, then, for Faulkner, Romantic myth as both grand, lyrical evocation and ideologically charged re-presentation of the past. We have as well myth as object lesson, prophesy, code of conduct, faith, epistemology, and decorum—in the mode of William Blake and his successors. Additionally, there is modern myth—critically encoded by Eliot to describe Joyce's continuous, formally eloquent paralleling of time past and time present. All of these, I think, work their formal course in Faulkner's oeuvre. Having taken up residence on that "little patch of Mississippi"—what he called his own "little postage stamp of native soil"—recommended by Anderson, and drawing on contemporaries from Romantics to moderns, Faulkner turned multiple deployments of myth to brilliant fictional advantage.

Who, then, are his contemporaries? I hazard the response that his contemporaries are all who occupy and creatively challenge the same mythical time/space that Faulkner inhabited as a southerner and an American, a white American born into strange racial economies, a man of the New World who dared tally the accounts of humanity's responsibility to a holy errand into the wilderness. Faulkner's contemporaries, one might say, are those who recognize and do what they can to emulate his own prolific labors with a southern past, as well as his ethical and prophetic wrestlings with the state and possibilities of humanity's future. Those who share—in another common sense of "contemporary"—Faulkner's modernity do so because they, like he, dare as readers and as ethical, fair-minded contemporary interpreters to enter with him into furious contest with and dreadful excavation of the past of the Americas. The McCaslins of *The Bear* know how taxing that past can be. We listen to them ruminating as follows:

> "So this land is, indubitably, of and by itself cursed," and he
> "Cursed." . . . that whole edifice intricate and complex and
> founded upon injustice and erected by ruthless rapacity
> and carried on even yet with at times downright savagery
> not only to the human beings but the valuable animals
> too, yet solvent and efficient and, more than that: not only
> still intact but enlarged, increased; brought still intact by
> McCaslin, himself little more than a child then, through

and out of the debacle and chaos of twenty years ago where hardly one in ten survived.

Curses and adoration reappear. The real bond, I think, between Faulkner and those who would be contemporary with him resides in a common dedication to the well-wrought representation and just moral judgment of the mythic encounter with the pastness (which is also, of course, the presentness of modernity's transatlantic rupture) of the Americas.

I think of Faulkner less as an author than as a journey, a mythic and always contemporary encounter waiting, like an interpretive stone, to mark our "modernity." To mark modernity especially with respect to what we have made of an American South and its outrageous economies of race. To travel with Faulkner and engage him at every step with contemporary questions is to discover, I think, what promises of modernism we have kept and which others we have tragically broken. An argument can be made that only Richard Wright among our twentieth-century authors has issued a summons as profoundly relevant to such a journey through the "South" as William Faulkner. Hence, in the spirit and mode of Faulkner himself, I want to set out in what follows selective contours of my own mythic journey and encounter with, through, in awe of, and, yes, at times, in furious repudiation of Faulkner. I write as a black American, one born in the South, and now middle-aged, academic, literary-critical. What follows is a weave of mythic encounters with Faulkner. It is only myth because encounters with Faulkner are always overwritten by forces larger than ourselves, for us both useful and dangerous, seductive and simple. My journey is designed not to bore. It is a contemporary southerner's tale of one of our region's most furious mythographers. It is memoir from a black man who does not hate the South.

##

It was the summer of 1957 in Louisville, Kentucky, and the Compsons were going crazy.

> "Taint no luck on this place," Roskus said. The fire rose and fell behind him and Versh, sliding on his and Versh's face.

Dilsey finished putting me to bed. The bed smelled like
T. P. I liked it.
"What you know about it." Dilsey said. "What trance
you been in."
"Don't need no trance." Roskus said. "Ain't the sign of it
laying right there on that bed. Ain't the sign of it been here
for folks to see fifteen years now."

My father said: "You. You should have known better. Michael's older.
But he's not from around here. It was you who should have known
better."
    The bicycles glinted in the sweltering day. Sweat was pouring off
our faces as the man behind the counter said: "Y'all can get them here.
But you can't drink 'em at the counter."
    "Why?" said Michael. He was the nephew of a friend of my mother's
who lived in Detroit. "Why can't we drink them here? The place is
empty."
    "Jes can't. We don't never serve y'all in the front, neither at the
counter."
    The door leading to the kitchen swung open. The colored woman
walked right up behind us seated at the counter and said: "You boys
know you can't drink at this counter. You boys come on with me to
the back. It's cool back there. I got a table."
    Michael had the money. He paid for the milkshakes. The table
was an unwieldy chopping block. She pulled up two sturdy chairs.
She said: "You all must be crazy. There ain't no need for you to be in
here. You could'a gone to Page's up on Chestnut Street if you wanted
ice cream. Drink them things quick and get on out of this kitchen.
It's enough I gotta be here."
    My father said: "Michael is visiting, but you live here. You should
have known better than to drink in anybody's kitchen. This is the
South. You should have known better. Don't ever do that again."
    Then my brother came home from Fisk University. He was
different from when he left. He said there were all sorts of "incredible"—that was his word, "incredible"—things going on in
the South where he had been in school all year. He said he and
his friends were working with a famous man who gave the most

beautiful "orations"—that was his word—he had ever heard. His name was "King."

It was 1957, and I asked my older brother what King "orated" about, and he said "freedom" for colored people in the South. "What about the South?" I asked him. My older brother said: "You should know better. You live here." Then he gave me a book called *The Sound and the Fury.* "Here," he said. "Read this. Everything is changing in the South."

I didn't ride my bicycle for three days. I was going into the ninth grade in the fall. I sat on top of the long, full bookcases my mother's father had built in the big room on the third floor and read this book my older brother gave me by William Faulkner. It was a crazy book. The image/feeling of Benjy the idiot "bellering" and seeming to love the smell of rain made me nauseated. Luster, and Roskus, and T. P., and Dilsey—all funny-sounding colored people—almost didn't register at all. I had no working knowledge of them. Perhaps because television was but two years old in our household, and very controlled. Perhaps because my parents were not partisans of minstrelsy. I did recognize Dilsey's church at the end of the book. I had been there. Was that grotesque of a preacher "orating" like my brother's King? I wondered. But the white people were the major players. At least I thought so, and I couldn't for the life of me figure out what muddy drawers had to do with anything, had to do with the South, or me and Michael. I should have known better. I hated "Miss Cahline" and Jason. Quentin and Caddy's breathless, incestuous touching brought adolescent response along my pulses.

"Well, did you read it?" my brother asked. "Yes," I answered. "What's it about, then?" he asked. "Crazy people. But what's that got to do with the South?" He laughed.

I was from the "here"—the South of my father's chastisement. I should have known better. I might have known what was signified by the sound and the fury. I had seen the sign White Waiting Room at the train station. I was one of the colored pioneers who integrated "white schools" full of people who regarded us like we were Luster and T. P. and alien forever.

"Go on." T. P. said. "Holler again. I going to holler myself. Whooey." Quentin kicked T. P. again. He kicked T. P. into

the trough where the pigs ate and T. P. lay there. "Hot dog."
T. P. said. "Didn't he get me then. You see that white man
kick me that time. Whooey."

I should have known better. But one's natal geography is so deep,
so saturated in the flesh and consciousness—fitting, as the artist Zora
Neale Hurston felicitously phrased the matter, "like a tight chemise."
It is "here" and "home" and "our town" and "my city," but never,
at least in adolescence (a well-fed, mind you, and loved and shel-
tered adolescence), never a territory requiring map and compass.
Orations and ideology and history and race relations and plantations
and slavery were not the curriculum of my boyhood. There was no
burden of racial memory foisted upon me. What derived then from
the South as geography early on was only the stifling fear and foreknowledge that came—usually inexplicably—when told: "We don't
serve y'all in the front, neither at the counter." I wish I had known
better. Faulkner was no help at all.

Only years later did I learn that what I, of course, required most
desperately was a myth of my own—as I had learned from William
Blake as early as my graduate school days at UCLA—through which
to engage the parallel time of the South (past and present) and to
release me from the bondage of incomprehension before that red-
olent myth of another, namely, Mr. Faulkner. Though there was
certainly an implicit southern dread—an actual terror yet to be
discovered—in what transpired at the counter, in the newly integrated schools of Louisville, and at rallies and boycotts that my older
brother was attending in Tennessee, I didn't yet know the longer
story rooted in the land of my birth. Did not even have a notion
that the instantaneity of impression made by a mentally ill Benjy on
my adolescent consciousness was part of a grand myth made by Mr.
Faulkner—one with which I would have to come to my own terms
of order and understanding. Only later, then, did I recognize some
clear contemporaneity with the sole proprietor of Yoknapatawpha
County. In time, we might become regionalists, together.

I wish I had known better.

⁝⁝

King was no longer a remote name when the train deposited its Louisville contingent at Washington's Union Station on a sultry August evening in 1961. King was elaborated and unfolding. A civil rights revolution had as leader Dr. Martin Luther King, Jr.—the Right Reverend Dr. Martin Luther King, Jr.—charismatic orator par excellence. The descendant whites of Yoknapatawpha were going completely crazy—bombs, arson, murder, beatings were standard fare in resistance to the colored thousands, those dark bodies and faces moving across landscapes and sites of old exclusion in the South, singing, "And before I'll be a slave / I'll be buried in my grave / And go home to my Lord / And be free."

The campus pals of Howard University met us and transported us to Charles Drew Hall to settle in for the larger education ahead. We boasted we were from the "Big L." We did not make claims to southern heritage, thinking we were hiply cosmopolitan. Louisville was, after all, the largest city in Kentucky. And we all knew Cassius Clay—homeboy, Olympic champion in Rome; he had partied with us, run track against us for Central High. We drafted his account for mythic status in our first Howard University comings and goings.

Then as term began, I walked through the door of a classroom drenched in September morning sun and saw one of the most beautiful brown-skinned women I had ever seen. Seated atop the desk, gorgeous legs showing from a dark skirt, and cream-colored sweater subtly décolleté. She was my humanities teacher. Her bearing was that of an oracle.

I took up residence on the front row. Seated next to me was a thin, impatient, intense brown-skinned young man who seemed to hum with energy. His hair was roughly curly, not short, smooth, and greased down like that of boys from the Big L.

We began. The text was William Faulkner's *The Bear*. I had read the book with the kind of Type A alacrity I brought by that time to all my studies. A lover of adventure stories who was always inventing backyard wildernesses, obstacles, challenges for myself, *The Bear*, a good hunting story, should have been simple for me. But the language kept getting in the way, and the characters seemed to be a single bundle—like those cartoon moments when rival forces are battling and one sees only a big cloud of dust with various arms, legs, hands, and faces pummeling about. Who was Sam Fathers? Why were he and Boon clamored into the same breath? What was Major de Spain a "major" of? What did Old Ben really "symbolize"?

The beautiful, appropriately histrionic, honey-voiced humanities teacher worked to help me out. She explained that this was a bildungsroman. I wrote that down. A tale of the coming of age of a young man. "Ike McCaslin," she said, "has to journey into the wilderness hands free—no gun, no compass—in order to understand the grandeur of his heritage." She went on, saying: "Sam Fathers, the bear, the great gun-metal-blue dog, Lion, are forces teaching young McCaslin humility and courage before forces and powers larger than his single life." I continued writing. And then a voice broke across the honeyed stream of the teacher's speaking, demanding:

> Why are we reading the work of an old cracker southern white man anyway? Isn't this a Negro university? Aren't Negroes today doing everything they can—marching and boycotting and integrating schools—to get us rid of people just like this old Mississippi cracker we are paying so much attention to today? We ought to be reading Mao Zedong. We ought to be in the streets of Cambridge, Maryland. We ought to be helping out Dr. King!

His voice grew more fiercely declamatory with each pronouncement. His eyes more intense. It was the young man with roughly curly hair. He was staring now at the teacher.

"Mr. Carmichael," she said (for it was Stokely Carmichael who was seated beside me):

> There are times and places—as I am certain you know and as Scripture dictates—for all things. To everything, there is a season. Here, in my class at Howard University, on this day, it is time for Faulkner. Besides, Mr. Carmichael, if you read *all* of *The Bear*, you might be surprised. You might even find in it something to help you help Dr. King.

The last she delivered with a smile that suggested endless possibilities.

I was enamored by Professor Morrison's response (for it was Toni Morrison who first taught me the humanities). She was a Faulkner advocate. Six years before that classroom exchange, she had written in her master's thesis for Cornell University:

> In *The Bear* . . . there is a description of Sam Fathers as a man who "had learned humility through suffering and learned pride through the endurance which survived suffering." The call for humility and endurance is familiar enough in Faulkner's works to suggest a credo, and it is precisely these qualities that Quentin does not have. Though he suffers he does not learn humility.

Stokely Carmichael was silenced. Like me, he read all of *The Bear*. But in the bourgeois provinces of 1961 Howard University, I am not certain any of us understood the connection—the mythic solidarity—between the mere hunting story of the work's initial offering and the tale of the awful ledgers that occupies the work's closing. "Comparative slavery" was not on the course list for the fall term of 1961 at Howard University, the "capstone of Negro education." In fact, I think there were many like me who had no idea of the holocaustal horror that was our American past. Toni Morrison did all she could to induct us into the myth of suffering, humility, guilt, and expiation that William Faulkner had crafted to illuminate America's regions of servitude. But we were so awfully young. How—even in the continuing stages of our own conscientious and ambitious efforts to "redeem" the land of cotton—could we make sense of the type of gigantic, horrible egos that Faulkner mythically set before us? "Who else," ask the McCaslins,

> could have declared a war against a power with ten times the area and a hundred times the men and a thousand times the resources, except men who could believe that all necessary to conduct a successful war was not acumen nor shrewdness nor politics nor diplomacy nor money nor even integrity and simple arithmetic but just love of land and courage.

Who else, indeed—but those who have corrupted a God-bequeathed and incorruptible wilderness with their possessive design, their unfeeling egos driven to make the wondrous world into *things*, to make all into a thing? Life becomes trivialized and disgustingly reduced to stakes in a poker game by men who do not take the wilderness to heart, but take it—saw mill and railroad girder and switch engine and razor-edged axe crashing into timber—take it, read it as possible possession to be scratched at and scratched at until it yields currency. Such men leave ledgers, records, whole libraries of inscribed guilt to be reckoned with by subsequent generations.

> Uncle Buddy had won Tomey's Terrel's wife Tennie in the poker-game of 1859—"possible strait against three Treys in sight Not called"—; no pale sentence or paragraph scrawled in cringing fear of death by a weak and trembling hand as a last desperate sop flung backward at retribution, but a Legacy, a Thing, possessing weight to the hand and bulk to the eye and even audible.

The Bear's concluding journey of young Isaac—son of the fathers, bearer of the weight of countless generations, biblical in his exchanges with his cousin McCaslin the elder—the journey concludes, as do so many sober paragraphs of Faulknerian myth, with madness. Boon and the squirrels. The scene swells with belated, screaming protection for that which is already doomed, forever dishonored by the offices of southern life.

Toni Morrison labored—against a backdrop of white southerners' rabid resistance, rage, rape, and vilifying rhetoric against civil rights—to teach us Faulkner's use value and mythic potential for seeking our own knowledge and redemption with respect to economies that were still holding us in desperate fee.

> Apparently they can learn nothing save through suffering, remember nothing save when underlined in blood.

If Toni Morrison could not—as no person can—bestow upon us a myth of our own, she was still patently aware of what language and the moral wrestling of grand myth looks like. And she urged us—even Stokely Carmichael—not to judge the old Mississippian by his fall but by his mythically heroic prose, wrestling with what humans had done to each other—and to all the earth and the animals entrusted by God to their keeping.

After such knowledge, what myths of redemption and forgiveness could we forge?

⠶

We had lived in Paris—my wife, my infant son, and I—long enough for me to feel entirely confident about finding my way to the branch of the Sorbonne where I was scheduled to lecture to a seminar of French students on Faulkner's long short story "Wash." Professor Marie Claire Vanderest had asked, upon learning that I hailed from the American South, if I liked Faulkner. Truth to tell, since my course with Professor Morrison and a brief, disastrous encounter with *Light in August* in graduate school, I had not given the Mississippi writer a thought. I had not discovered—nor was I really concerned to discover—my southern contemporaneity with him. In fact, I had labored mightily to bring about that successful affectation of accent and personal bearing (not unlike Addison Gayle, Jr.) that would completely disguise my southernness. I was a Dr. now, a Ph.D. who had shared institutional space with Cleanth Brooks, Rene Wellek, R. W. B. Lewis, and Harold Bloom. What had I to do with the South, or the South with me? I was in my own version of Parisian exile for a year, living in Antony and riding the Linge de Sceaux into Paris's Luxembourg Gardens, taking in the Latin Quarter, strolling about where Joyce and Wright and Hemingway and Baldwin had taken their leave. Did I "like" Faulkner? Well, certainly not!

But who would—especially in French exile—scruple at an invitation to speak at the Sorbonne? Not I. Of course when Professor Vanderest named the text she wished me to elucidate, I swallowed hard. Uh . . . "Wash" . . . what was that? I asked her to send me a copy of the text so that I would be, as it were, on the same page with her students. She agreed to do so. And when the bulky sheaf of pages in photocopy arrived, I sat down immediately and commenced reading.

I was bowled over, enthralled, knocked back on my literary-critical heels, astonished by the world and its inhabitants who were washing over me like some savage Mississippi flood, pulverizing deltas of provinciality. It was an ocean of passions of race and rage, miscegenation and moral innocence. I had never, never in my comings and goings among texts encountered anyone remotely akin to Colonel Thomas Sutpen, sole proprietor of Sutpen's Hundred.

The awe of the title character, Wash Jones (while ethically naïve and self-destructive), in some ways expresses my own astonishment at Sutpen. Says Wash: "A fine proud man. If God Himself was to come down and ride the natural earth, that's what He would aim to look like." This of Sutpen galloping on his black stallion across his hundred acres wrested from the wilderness. This of a man Wash factors as "his own lonely apotheosis" and white supremacist "self-defense" against his own mean, poor-white caste status in a South where Negroes are better spoken, clothed, fed, and cared for than Wash Jones.

By the time I encountered Colonel Sutpen, I had shared space with the exalted white academics (Bloom & Co.) at Yale aforementioned—but in New Haven my most dedicated labors (something I have already hinted at) had been to the kind of self-reinvention that is American. I had gone in a shot from tweed-coated "good Negro professor" to African dashiki–wearing "bad revolutionary new black man." The poster on my Yale office wall—purchased at Mr. Micheaux's famous 125th Street and Lenox Avenue bookstore in Harlem—had black fists raised and read *The Ultimate Solution Is Black Revolution!*

To change the order of things, we needed black studies. We needed Black Power. We needed black nationalist institutions of our own—books and journals, schools, and a literary and cultural critique of our own. My hair was wildly rough and curly now. My eyes were always striving for intensity. Most important, my mind had commenced to absorb the shadows and acts, accountings and reckonings, narratives and powerful lyrics of a black past that had never been disappeared *tout court* by the United States, but was only invisible in that marketplace ignored by a kind of general, white, academic gentleman's agreement.

Nothing there to buy, right?
And he: *No, nothing.*

W. E. B. Du Bois, James Baldwin and Benjamin Quarles, Frantz Fanon, Gwendolyn Brooks, Alain Locke and Langston Hughes, Ralph Ellison, Gil Scott-Heron, the Last Poets and Nina Simone, Ed Bullins, Amiri Baraka, Sonia Sanchez, James Weldon Johnson, and Arna Bontemps . . . merchants and prophets and apostles and sapient sutlers of the orishas and loas all . . . an African and Afro-American festival of rare and generous gifts of a transatlantic dark spirit's survival and flourishing. *When the revolution comes. When the revolution comes!* No, it won't be televised.

I read "Wash" and Colonel Sutpen against the backdrop of my mind-enhancing and spirit-expanding acquaintance with a South that had always been hiding inside my brown body, waiting to emerge. Here was Ole Sis Goose and Brer Rabbit and High John and Stackalee filling in the interstices of Faulkner's mythscapes. No longer were there only the visible, lamentable, or laudatory whites tragically worn—nor solely the taciturn, shambling, dissembling, enduring, comic, block-headed, parodic, pompous Negroes. When I read "Wash," a whole new world opened before me. For I now knew the other story of those Negroes who drove Mr. Wash Jones maddeningly and buffoonishly—in a wretched triumph of "race pride"—to sacrifice his own granddaughter to the "rutting" of Sutpen.

Wash Jones was less undone by a passive well-keptness of "Negroes" than by the fear of what I came to know as Afro-America's ineluctable dynamism—a brilliant black creativity (even if no more than of character and resistance) made out of bare bones and spare rags. Wash realized his being as epiphenomenon—a sad secondariness to the ruthless exclusionism of his dreamed apotheosis, Colonel Thomas Sutpen. And though Wash claims an awful vengeance for his own stupidly racialized episteme, he can never quite eradicate the boomeranging outrageousness of the colonel's brutally casual first response to the child (the daughter) he has fathered (with Wash's total complicity) upon the granddaughter: "Well, Milly too bad you're not a mare. Then I could give you a decent stall in the stable." All that scuppernong harbor *amité* between Wash and the colonel come roaring up the poor white's esophagus like flushed bile. Time's chosen healer, Wash takes scythe in hand and slays the man who arrived in Jefferson, at his second showing, with twenty "wild niggers" and a French architect.

I was able to grasp the grandeur—and the severe limitations—of Faulkner's driving myth in that year of 1972 because I had my own necessary background of black and southern history. A myth of my own in formation. I took up the larger story with Faulkner's majestic achievement in *Absalom, Absalom!* And knowing the whole story—as Faulkner saw it—I set out by metro for the Seventh Arrondissement of Paris to lecture to French students.

Of course, Faulkner had done Paris long before. He was a shy writer in exile, afraid to speak to James Joyce. But he drank the Left Bank café rounds nonetheless.

The metro offered a perfect ride and—*comme à l'habitude*—was resolutely on time. I strolled the few blocks to Paris 7 rehearsing the rituals and rhetoric of the Faulknerian revelation I would bring to these French students. My grasp of the materials seemed secure, particularly buttressed by my handsomely acquired and shining new black studies insights.

About a block from the campus, I was drawn up by scores, upon scores, upon scores, of riot-gear-clad French police troops—and rings and rings of black mariahs (those awesome carriers and incarceration vans that put one strongly in mind of tumbrels—and Foucault). There had been a mini-riot at Paris 7 that morning. The university was on lock-down. It was still true that the aftershocks and revolutionary and incendiary spirit of Mai Soixante-huit were shaking the city of Balzac and Zola. Would Faulkner have understood this continental and youth-led *Je refuse*—this demotic repudiation of old aristocratic arrangements of things? Perhaps. But one doubts he would have sympathized with its earlier dark-complexion stirrings with Algerians, or its new millennial energies (as of today) in the vast immigrant arrivals and strivings that gave Jean-Marie Le Pen such a boost from rabid whites in 2002 elections in France.

I found Marie Claire. She suggested we take our show to a local café. We did. The students, I am convinced, were far more serious about their steaming cups of espresso and public café attitudes than about Mr. Wash Jones and Colonel Thomas Sutpen, whom I labored mightily—with all the mythical acumen I could muster—to bring clearly before their eyes.

"*This is America,*" I wanted to scream at them. "*This is the America of a South I am coming to know. It is a South forever and already changed by the mind and souls of black folk. Colonel Sutpen is dead—and yet never more mythically alive than at this revolutionary moment.*"

I hear Wash Jones inquiring, "The mought have kilt us, but they aint whipped us yit, air they?" And I don't need Sutpen or anyone else to say for me: "For *America's* sake, let us certainly hope you are whipped forever." Not through war and pillage and carnage on the field but by our construction of an accessible path to the invisible marketplace where our black and impulsive voices have always been.

Thus sadly musing. "Thus sadly musing," writes Du Bois of his train journey back to Nashville from the "behind the mountains" place where he witnessed the demise of the beautiful Josie's ambitions to live a larger life. My metro return to Antony was nothing so dramatic. But I did know that I was rendered by the experiences of that day forever a contestatory American contemporary of that fellow southerner Faulkner, who was white, brilliant, male, and I know now, heroically limited.

░░

In the '80s I taught *Absalom, Absalom!* to Ivy League students—black and white—and found such dead space as would amaze you. They so much more appreciated Mark Twain and his remarkable twins. Perhaps they were as baffled as I once had been (way back in my early days, perched upon those grandfather-built bookcases) by the utter craziness of the families of Yoknapatawpha. It was the Reagan/Bush era. And maybe these students felt Faulkner was simply too old school to count, despite my feverish, moralizing, histrionic urgings to discussion and debate. "Aren't you concerned about the history of the South?" I asked them, only to see blank stares. Of course, I now see that my failure was to register my own discoveries as the opening gambit to teaching Faulkner. I did not share with them my journey. And—most important—I did not alert them to the fact that I repudiated—and repudiated utterly—the enormous failings of the author from Oxford.

⸬

Earlier, I mentioned my disastrous graduate school encounter with *Light in August*. Let me explain. I was the only black person in an American literature graduate seminar of fifty students in the balmy, West Coast venue of UCLA during the mid-1960s. Dr. Martin Luther King was unstoppably on the march. Civil rights and voting rights bills had become law of the land. My father had left Louisville and become a major player in public health in the nation's capital. I had won a fellowship for graduate study.

And then came *Light in August* with its feverish, homicidal, laborious, racialized syllables of purest bizarrerie: "surrounded by the summer smell and the summer voices of invisible negroes. . . . On all sides, even within him, the bodiless fecundmellow voices of Negro women murmured. It was as though he and all other manshaped life about him had been returned to the lightless hot wet primogenitive Female." There is more: "Then he told her. 'I got some nigger blood in me'" (196).

Again, listen: "He now lived as man and wife with a woman who resembled an ebony carving. At night he would lie in bed beside her . . . trying to breathe into himself the dark color, the dark and inscrutable thinking and being of Negroes, with each suspiration trying to expel from himself the white blood and the white thinking and being" (225–226).

And we are not—nor will we ever be—finished hearing the feverish, awful nightmare of our southern mythographer's disaster of a novel that is, finally, not about anything—at least not about anything real, save perhaps prurient, disastrous myths of black blood and odor, Negro razors and bovine stupidity, white nymphomania and black male lasciviousness, militaristic white desire sublimated into grim and unlikely castration.

Oh yes, and this is in a single novel that I was called upon to explicate for that graduate seminar of interested whites. *"Mr. Faulkner,"*

I wanted to scream, *"how could you do this to me?"* But I didn't even know—then—that is what I wanted to scream. I was made ill—physically ill—by the pandering to white American racism and deeply mentally ill fantasies that are *Light in August*. Stokely was—at least where this novel is concerned—correct about William Faulkner being an old Mississippi cracker.

Of course, *Light in August* is merely the most offensive of Faulkner's mythological errors. Ashley Montagu calls race America's "most dangerous myth." And the novelist from Oxford was not always the most careful person in avoiding the pitfalls of the dangerous myth. His miscegenatory underpinnings and overlays for plot, theme, and motif are often grandiosely bereft of any known objective correlative. The sound and fury about Joe Christmas's "bloodlines" are disastrously silly, as are some of the purple prose passages rendered to Charles Bon and the octoroons of New Orleans.

How profound a historical fact is it—after the exemplary work of a new African American literary and cultural studies that has provided new ways of reading, new histories, new criteria of evaluation, new tools of analysis—that white men who had all power, on armed plantations, brutally raped black women and gave life to second "colored families"? While many years ago I might have been shocked (or enlightened, as the case actually was) by such matters, certainly a graduate professor of American literature four decades ago and surely at the present time should not find such matters more than clichés. There is, of course, as my opening discussion of myth for the present reflections make clear, a vast critical distance and difference between stereotypes (especially banal ones) and mythic inventiveness striving for systems of interpretation and strides toward modernity. And we certainly can never again, I hope, be titillated or obsessed with such matters in the manner of *Light in August*. The positive fecundity and grandeur of Faulkner's mythmaking indeed flounders in the prurience of his *Light in August* fascinations: "when [Bon said he was a 'Negro,' white men] believed he lied in order to save his skin, or worse: from sheer besotment of sexual perversion, in either case the result was the same: the man with the body and limbs almost as light and delicate as a girl's giving the first blow" (167).

Within the same world of titillation and stereotype, a clumsily characterized Joe Christmas takes it upon himself to kick the living daylights out of a Negro girl whom he is complicit in gang raping. And with all those classics and philosophy books in his library, no less, Faulkner plays the racist pulp fictionist. He should have known better. In a contemporary reading, he seems only to be a victim of the rankest fantasy of white patriarchs: that they have open license to the sexuality of a putatively bounden and dark Other.

In such failed moments of Faulkner as *Light in August*, it comes as pathetic explanation and sad commentary to know that he was— from an early age—a chronic alcoholic, and in later life an abuser of narcotics and alcohol who endured the horrific therapy of electroshock and wandered from sanitarium to sanitarium—cheating death by only momentary clean-and-sober intervals. (Madness, too, has the South as its real, horrific metaphor.) Despite the purely secular bizarrerie and pathological explanation for it of such racist slippages as *Light in August* and other Faulknerian texts, there remains—strong as ever in some instances—a white (and, yes, in these days, a black) literary-critical and culturally critical demiurge to *save* Faulkner and his work from their own racial failings. It is as though Wash Jones— having discovered the mad megalomania and unfeeling indifference of Colonel Sutpen—decides not to slay the dragon, but to find a symbology—or an excuse—to proclaim everything Sutpen ever did represented a labor of indisputable "greatness."

For example, there is a reading of *Light in August* that suggests the novel represents Christian allegory. Because Joe Christmas receives his name from a white orphanage when he is delivered to its doors at Christmas, critics wish to see Joe's birth as the resonant figuration of the virgin birth of Jesus Christ. Given Christ's genealogy and the utterly un-orphaned state of his birth, where do such critical postulates about Christmas come from? Does a strange impulse to find in the novel's substitution of a seasonal nominative for "Doe" produce the confusion? Again, when a salvation-of-Faulknerian-greatness criticism attempts to read Joe's last days as a figuration of Christ's Passion—which is sacramental, characterized by conviviality, discipleship, generosity, outgoing acceptance of the world and of his fate to redeem it—what are they thinking? Joe, in his last days, is mentally distraught (ill?), hermetic in extremis, wearing "Negro shoes," from which (in perhaps one of the novel's more outrageous moments) he seems to absorb an essentialist, Negro "racial essence." (This is not unlike Lena Grove in her "men's shoes." And of course, Lena is the novel's real, sympathetic protagonist—even in all the misogyny of the narrator's commentary on "woman." Lena's story is certainly more compellingly, artistically, and authentically rendered than Joe's.) Christ perishes in resounding redemption of a sinful world—with a free willingness and a barely comprehensible sacrifice. By contrast, Joe forever reminds us of the South's most brutish moral obtuseness. He is victim to that dread practice of southern spectacle lynching. He represents, in one view, certainly not Christ, but the most heinous of southern sins for which only Christ's mercy might atone.

Light in August is not a powerful, successful, or redeemable allegory that artistically brings together the lives of Christ and Joe Christmas. I think only a ham-fisted salvation-of-greatness weds Joe and Jesus. *Light in August* is, perhaps, a racist parody from the pen of a southern author who suffered tremens of self-medication all his life. But it is not an artistic or achieved allegory—at least where race in America is concerned. The question then abides: "Mr. Faulkner, how could you do this to us?"

⁘

So how, then, do we sum up an Afro-American contemporaneity with the sage of Yoknapatawpha?

We say, I think, that he is always the Cerberus at the gateway of a southern landscape. We cannot experience America without encountering him in the specificity of his biography and in the mythological South he conjured. He is also the avatar and mythic craftsman of so many undead ghosts of our national imaginings. "What did you do?" we ask.

> What did you do to enable yourselves exclusively to be called the only true Americans, further to deem yourselves

speakers and possessors of the land's only native language
and natural wonders? What did you—all locked, as you are,
into the consensus of whiteness—do to assume the rights
of denying and incarcerating, flaying, raping, and murder-
ing with a flattering word all who do not look like you?

Faulkner's mythic answer is closely akin to my own. The "you"
of white patriarchy murdered, maimed, polluted, and hammered
out legal accords of a brutal American exclusivity that still threatens
the planet with mass destruction in the name of "democracy" and
"honor." The imperiousness of the *you*, Faulkner claims, is purchased,
only at the price of the most catastrophic betrayal of the ethical and
humane possibilities of the New World as a fruitful "refuge and
sanctuary of liberty and freedom from the old world's worthless
evening."

While my own contemporary black studies mythography would
suggest that Faulkner's vision of expatiation and redemption for a
flagrantly uncharitable white patriarchal possessiveness accords too
much passivity to "the Negro," my emerging myth of origins and
new southern promise suggests that Faulkner got his agents right.
He knew Afro-Americans provided not only the music of southern spheres but also the complicating energies of those spheres'
revolutions. Richard Wright proclaimed, "The Negro is America's
metaphor." The mythic Faulkner proclaimed possibilities of modal
salvation from black Americans because of that ineffable ability to
endure—in humility and courage and self-understanding and outgoing embrace of humanity's awful incumbencies. Faulkner knew
Afro-Americans possessed "what they got not only not from white
people but not even despite white people because they had it already
from the old free fathers a longer time free than us because we have
never been free." Thus speaks Ike McCaslin near the conclusion of
The Bear.

Would it not be delightful to have the Toni Morrison of *Playing in
the Dark* and William Faulkner of that great wilderness short story in
the same room discussing the merits of the Mississippian's proph-
esied relief for monumental American moral failures?

I think so.

But such a prospect of two so-removed geniuses in conversation in the same academic rooms carries us out of myth and into fantasy. It is time to stop with a French paraphrase of an American presidential moment long past. If asked again—even in the hot dread of his ranting southern lucubrations—if I was, indeed of the party of the old Mississippian, I would have to answer—with all the complexity of my black, southern being: *Moi, je suis un Faulknerian!*

*"If you see Robert Penn Warren, ask him: Who **does** speak for the Negro?"*

REFLECTIONS ON MONK, BLACK WRITING,
AND PERCIVAL EVERETT'S *Erasure*

DE KOONING: You put your name on it.

RAUSCHENBERG: Why not? It's my work.

DE KOONING: Your work? Look at what you've done to my picture.

RAUSCHENBERG: Nice job, eh? It was a lot of work erasing it. My wrist is still sore. I call it "Erased Drawing."

DE KOONING: That's very clever.

RAUSCHENBERG: I've already sold it for ten grand.

DE KOONING: You sold my picture?

RAUSCHENBERG: No, I erased your picture. I sold my erasing.

—Percival Everett, *Erasure*

I'm not thinking that race thing now; it's not on my mind. Everybody's trying to get me to think it, though, but it doesn't bother me. It only bugs the people who are trying to get me to think it.

—Valerie Wilmer, "Monk on Monk," *Downbeat* (1965)

I could shake the nation for a while with a crime or with indecent disclosures, but my pride lies in earning the right to call myself, quite simply, *writer.*

—Ralph Ellison, "The World and the Jug"

I would wish rather to suggest that the alleged derivativeness of writing, however real and massive, was possible only on one condition: that the "original," "natural," etc. language had never existed, never been intact and untouched by writing, that it had itself always been a writing. An archewriting . . .

—Jacques Derrida, *Of Grammatology*

Stackalee went with the devil's wife and his girlfriend, too.
Winked at the devil and said, I'll go with you.
The devil turned around to hit him a lick.
Stackalee knocked the devil down with a big black stick.
Now, to end this story, so I heard tell,
Stackalee, all by his self, is running hell.

—"Stackalee," traditional ballad

It is a twice-told tale among readers and critics that Faulkner struggled mightily for American recognition as an artist. His subjects seemed too baroque, his prose too convoluted, his insights about the South too difficult to find in a tangled forest of symbols, plot shifts, and an ever-expanding genealogy of characters. It was not until the 1940s that Faulkner got his artistic due through the timely efforts of Malcolm Cowley. Cowley edited and published to popular acclaim *The Portable Faulkner*, which included a brilliant introductory guide to the master. Faulkner, who had already begun to enjoy considerable European acclaim, was thus fixed forever as a southern writer. A decade later he received the Nobel Prize for literature.

This "fixing" of both literature and author is a familiar critical phenomenon, which always has to be undone as years roll by. That is to say, what is held to be typically *anything*—whether "English," "southern," or "black American" literature—will always be unfixed, unsettled, challenged, and resituated by subsequent generations.

This seems especially true with regard to the workings of literature and literary criticism in what might be called a *black American southern expressive tradition.*

Richard Wright's rise to fame and literary stardom as a black American writer was built upon a southern foundation, and Wright's insights and injunctions come to us as sharp analysis, thunderous polemic, and unyielding protest. His first novel, *Native Son*—about a black youngster whose family migrates from the South to Chicago after his father is lynched—stunned the white American and black American literary worlds of readers, critics, reviewers, and social analysts. Wright was crowned king of the hill with respect to what was then known as "Negro literature." Later, it was the ambitious and brilliant black prose stylist James Baldwin (who decidedly was *not* a southern writer) who unsettled Wright's crown and worked critically to take possession of the hill. In his essays "Everybody's Protest Novel" and "Many Thousands Gone," Baldwin condemns unequivocally what, it might be argued, is the black southern formalism of Wright's most famous work, *Native Son.* If Faulkner was too convoluted and difficult to fathom, Wright was, for Baldwin, too angry, facile, and sociologically clichéd to provide any helpful understanding of the "black situation" in America. He did not capture, as writers must, the subtlety and nuance of black life as it was actually lived in America. Baldwin sensed that the literary and artistic craftsmanship necessary to capture such subtleties existed in two locales only in the 1950s: in "Negro music" and in the recently published prose of a young Ralph Ellison.

It goes without saying, of course, that Baldwin believed the most effective, nuanced, and powerful forms of black expression—forms that would unfix the lofty standing of Wright—were his own. What Baldwin set in motion (and Ellison signed on to) can perhaps be termed an *experimental black expressive cultural project*—something that would be more modern, cosmopolitan, complex than the oeuvre of Wright. Baldwin even stooped—in his eulogy titled "Alas, Poor Richard"—to calling the southern black writer a "Mississippi pickaninny, quick, bright-eyed, and mischievous." This certainly sounds regressive enough, doesn't it? The black experimental, or black postmodern, in our era (by which I mean the 1960s to the present) has strived to actualize Baldwin's project, seeking to erase Wright's name from the honored rolls of cosmopolitan intellectual thought and fiction.

One is mindful, of course, that such unfixing, experimental black efforts proceed always under the gaze of white literary managers, judges, and watchers of "Negro complexity" of thought. Such complexity is deemed at its highest when the Negro does not sound, or write, or think like a Negro! At times, the result of the willing collaboration between black writers intent on being, at least, nonsouthern—and, at most, experimentally postmodern—and their white critics is almost too painful to bear.

We know, for example, that the Harlem Renaissance poet Melvin Tolson set out to prove that he could weave Negro life and themes into the obfuscating, allusive, interminable logics of a (white) high-modern poetry that would win the accolades of world-class (white) critics. Tolson believed that, if he achieved his ends, the Negro as writer would never be looked upon again as simply one who made southern-based protests or black quotidian beauty into "regional" or "racial" writing.

But, alas, despite cosmopolitan experimentalists, ad hominem eulogies, and shrewd, often quite accomplished waves of black post-modernist writing in recent years, it is Wright who endures. He is heard in small towns of Portugal and colossal metropolises of South Asia as a black American writer par excellence, one of the canniest black voices of the South ever heard.

I think one must turn to that uproarious decade of black expressive cultural flowering that was the Black Arts movement of the 1960s as a starting point for a survey of the contours of what might be termed the "Wright protocol"—and its detractors. Moving from the 1960s forward, we may be able to get a handle on the workings of southernness and its voice in the Afro-American literary tradition. We might also come more thoroughly to comprehend the various fixing and unfixing that marks the black American writer's forays into a supposedly nuanced universalism. I have to blame a great deal of my obsession and passion about these issues on the brilliant poet of the '60s Etheridge Knight—who, like too many others, was a striking black creative genius who died too soon.

During his robust days, Etheridge Knight—whose first volume was titled *Poems from Prison* (and endorsed by Gwendolyn Brooks)—used to end our telephone conversations with the tag line: "And, Houston, if you see Robert Penn Warren, ask him: Who *does* speak for the Negro?"

I ran into Mr. Warren only once. It was in the 1980s in Louisiana, at a rather tame and sober occasion. Mr. Warren was being honored, yet because his vision was failing, he was unable to read his own poems. He had to yield the podium to a stand-in performer. I sat next to him at the head table, and it never crossed my mind to pose Etheridge's question.

Alas, Etheridge Knight, Robert Penn Warren, and Gwendolyn Brooks have all passed on. And somehow the vigorous irony of Knight's inquiry does not resonate in this new century as it did in the last. Knight's reference was to the famous (or notorious, depending on where you stood in reference to the legitimacy of black cultural nationalism) volume titled, precisely, *Who Speaks for the Negro?* (1965). Edited by Warren, the collection caused a stir among black American spokespersons. Who, after all, was Robert Penn Warren to ask the question? He had taken his stand in the 1930s with the group of conservative, white, agrarian southerners who labeled themselves "the Fugitives" and who were anything but progressive in their views on "the Negro." In the 1960s, it was not simply the volume's editor that caused a stir but also the title question itself. "Who speaks for the Negro?" has produced perhaps more anxiety than any other inquiry among the African American writerly cadre in the United States. For the question—especially as it resonates from the pen of an eminent white southerner—seems to imply at least two things. First, in the decade of the 1960s, when we were moving energetically away from "*the* Negro," the notion of such a definite-articled person nevertheless held pride of place in a white American imaginary. Further, the question implied there was an "authentic" and "racially truthful" way to speak by and for this definitive Negro. "Who speaks for the Negro?" thus gestures toward what a famous Gwendolyn Brooks poem calls "the real thing"—the definite "Negro" article. Etheridge Knight cast more than one ironic glance at such retrogressive critical arrogance.

(As I end this last sentence, a song from the Thelonious Monk CD I just bought on Broad Street in Philadelphia—where it is numbingly cold—kicks in. It fills the sound space of my hotel room. I imagine Monk here, brusquely asking: "What's all this stuff about 'race' and 'Negroes' you writing, man? I don't go for that stuff. I ain't gonna be writing no 'freedom now suites' anytime soon." As I listen to the CD, I recognize the melodic flow of "Ruby, My Dear"—one of my all-time favorite jazz compositions. I had forgotten the piece was Thelonious Monk's! All these years, his music speaking for me, through me, without my recognition—poor me, poor Monk! The disk soon moves on to the next track, "Well You Needn't." Nice to get reacquainted with you, Mr. Monk.)

African Americans—especially African American writers—do not take well to being reduced to a single, authentic, "racially truthful" voice. We are a manifold and complex population, and we want to be represented as such. The question "Who speaks for the Negro?" does just the opposite. It assumes there is a single, authoritative, expressive voice of the Negro. The consequence of this assumption (which is actually a boldly insulting presumption) is that every black man, woman, or child who sets out to write or to be a writer in the United States must devote themselves and their work to speaking for and being that "Negro" voice. "I have not written about being a Negro at such length," says James Baldwin, "because I expect that to be my only subject, but only because it was *the gate I had to unlock before I could hope to write about anything else*" (*Notes of a Native Son*, my italics). The "Negro writer" is expected, first and foremost, to "sound" Negro, and then to plumb the depths of Negrodom in America. "Who speaks for the Negro?" mandates, therefore, a bizarre correlation between the color of one's skin and the expected character of one's speech. "Thank God!" a white host is reported to have proclaimed when Paul Laurence Dunbar arrived at her home for a reading. "He is black as night and no one will credit his Negro genius to white blood!"

(The CD continues to spin in my Philadelphia hotel room. Monk's dark fingers lie flat on the keys. I recall that once an interviewer demonstrated for Monk the "proper" hand position for playing the piano—fingers perched perpendicular to the keys—and

Monk responded with feigned wide-eyed wonder: "So that's how you're supposed to do it?" The funereal horns of "Monk's Mood" do a slow march. I suddenly remember that in college I took precise aim at my southern accent, linguistic barrels loaded. I was in love with a black woman from the North whose speech was totally unlike mine. [She thought I was buying laundry detergent for my car when I told her I was going to get some "all."] That was indeed "Straight No Chaser," as Monk would have read it. Not stopping in the name of love, but sounding out—like Monk—parallel devices for a love supreme.)

A Meditation on Monk

One might envision Thelonious Monk the musician. He has arrived three hours late for his first set at Minton's. He is doing his dance, arms and elbows akimbo, jutting like chicken wings, knees dipping. He bobs and pirouettes around the piano. Vibes and drums create a sonic pas de deux. "Monk's Dance," to invoke James Baldwin again: "unlocks the gate" of the cage of color—that prison house of phenotype that keeps certain forms and norms both locked down and aggregated forever.

Monk refused the phenotype. And his music became (and remains) a POW—certainly often MIA—in America's immemorial culture war. On these shores, it's a white thing. Alas! Monk's dance is a ritual disaggregation, a *parallel* movement, not proper and perpendicular. It is countercritical and epistrophic, not classical at all.

It is manifest in black fits and starts, stern refusals to yield to tradition or to be told how to play (or write). These refusals to yield constitute and shape themselves as experimental expression—a specifically black trial-and-error, improvisation, and breakaway idiosyncrasy. It happens "'Round Midnight," of course, in the soft whirling vortex of piano, bass, sax, and drums. It occurs in black music, long before African American writers catch up.

Thelonious Monk and James Baldwin do ultimately dance the same dance, however, as is evident in the latter's observation in his essay "Many Thousands Gone," "It is only in his music, which

Americans are able to admire because a protective sentimentality limits their understanding of it, that the Negro in America has been able to tell his story."

Which suggests that to disaggregate skin color and speech character where the definitive "Negro" is concerned—to unlock the gate of overdetermined critical expectations—one does not need to "burn but his books," as with Shakespeare's Caliban on Prospero, but simply to dance "Monk's Dance": his *music*.

∷

Etheridge Knight and I never had drinks and listened to jazz together. But I am willing to wager that, if we had, he would have told me the musicians got it right. It is not a matter of *print*, but a matter of *mind*. Knight committed all of his poems to memory—a radical necessity for expressive black inmates in America. He performed with full-bodied, dancing brilliance. What Knight wanted to form his combos around, his group dynamics of call-and-response, was, ironically, always invisible. The improvisational experimentalist Zora Neale Hurston delineated black creative tactics of the invisible in *Mules and Men*:

> The theory behind our tactics [can be stated as follows]: "The white man is always trying to know into somebody else's business. All right, I'll set something outside the door of my mind for him to play with and handle. *He can read my writing but he sho' can't read my mind*. I'll put this play toy in his hand, and he will seize it and go away. Then I'll say my say and sing my song." (my italics)

It's a matter of mind. The mind, for expressive men and women of color—men and women who take self-conscious aim at their *expected* accents—is its own place. It realizes that its usable means and ends must be nuanced, polysyllabic, ambivalent—parallel rather than perpendicular, with respect to the mainstream.

∷

Among African American writers (and would-be writers), Monk's dance does crazy, mind-altering, wondrously expressive things with the black invisible. And black writing's goal (in the spirit of Baldwin) is to "unlock the gate"—to make the music of the invisible. "If," said Etheridge, "you see Robert Penn Warren, ask him: who *does* speak for the Negro?" And here is Whitney Balliett of the *New Yorker*, in his obituary for Monk:

> [Monk's] improvisations were attempts to disguise his love of melody. [To cover up his sentimentality?] He clothed whatever he played with spindly runs, flatted notes, flatted chords, repeated single notes, yawning silences, and zig-zag rhythms. Sometimes he pounded the keyboard with his right elbow. His style protected him not only from his love of melody but from his love of the older pianists he grew out of—Duke Ellington and the stride pianists. All peered out from inside his solos, but he let them escape only as parody.

To counter the question "who speaks for the Negro?" you have to explore the invisible, which creates its own style of expression. And such exploration is never free from the dark dread of anxiety—producing, sometimes, (self-)willing "executioners." The affective and effective general good of the black majority can get lost, stolen, sold out, or brilliantly ignored in the halls of parody. Parody must, then, be read as a style and form, not only of cultural capital (no matter how nobly or experimentally it is clothed) but also as a form of capital punishment. Though parody may seem to emanate from a stylish desire to (in James Weldon Johnson's formulation) "unscrew the inscrutable," it is certainly, always and forever, an *anxious* form of expression. And it can, perhaps uncritically, punish the black mass body in the name of this profitably stylish, artistic eloquence.

Knight knew "the Negro" was infinitely parody-able. But he also knew that Robert Penn Warren and his ilk were largely responsible for that. Like Monk, Knight knew that a too-clever, self-absorbed, egotistical (or sycophantic) deployment of black tactics of the invisible against the notion of "the Negro" could morph and become, finally, a technique of capitally punishing the visible black masses.

Thus, Knight's sly smile and conversational tag line were meant not
to laugh *with* Warren at "the Negro" but performatively, ironically,
and brilliantly to chuckle *at* Warren, raising the invisible to defiant
music, dancing *with* the black majority, moving with aggressive
belligerence against the regnant politics of . . . *everything*.

I don't think Knight ever expected to speak for the Negro, or to
be mistaken for anything other than what he was—a Mississippi
black boy who from a prison cell heard and translated a black music
of invisibility.

The Idea of Ancestry

I

Taped to the wall of my cell are 47 pictures: 47 black
faces: my father, mother, grandmothers (1 dead), grand
fathers (both dead), brothers, sisters, uncles, aunts,
cousins (1st & 2nd), nieces, and nephews. They stare
across the space at me sprawling on my bunk. I know
their dark eyes, they know mine. I know their style,
they know mine. I am all of them, they are all of me;
they are farmers, I am a thief, I am me, they are thee.

I have at one time or another been in love with my mother,
1 grandmother, 2 sisters, 2 aunts (1 went to the asylum),
and 5 cousins. I am now in love with a 7 yr old niece
(she sends me letters written in large block print, and
her picture is the only one that smiles at me).

I have the same name as 1 grandfather, 3 cousins, 3 nephews,
and 1 uncle. The uncle disappeared when he was 15, just took
off and caught a freight (they say). He's discussed each year
when the family has a reunion, he causes uneasiness in
the clan, he is an empty space. My father's mother, who is 93
and who keeps the Family Bible with everybody's birth dates
(and death dates) in it, always mentions him. There is no
place in her Bible for "whereabouts unknown."

II

Each fall the graves of my grandfathers call me, the brown
hills and red gullies of Mississippi send out their electric
messages, galvanizing my genes. Last yr / like a salmon quitting
the cold ocean—leaping and bucking up his birthstream / I
hitchhiked my way from L.A. with 16 caps in my pocket and a
monkey on my back, and I almost kicked it with the kinfolks.
I walked barefooted in my grandmother's backyard / I smelled the old
land and the woods / I sipped cornwhiskey from fruit jars with
the men /
I flirted with the women / I had a ball till the caps ran out
and my habit came down. That night I looked at my grandmother
and split / my guts were screaming for junk / but I was almost
anointed / I had almost caught up with me.
The next day in Memphis I cracked a croaker's crib for a fix.

This yr there is a gray stone wall damming my stream, and when
the falling leaves stir my genes, I pace my cell or flop on my bunk
and stare at 47 black faces across the space. I am all of them,
they are all of me, I am me, they are thee, and I have no sons
to float in the space between.

1968

The stakes for Knight's implicit, shrewd, and ironic deconstruction
of Warren's 1960s prescriptive critical conservatism were extraordi-
narily high. One needs, then, to read Knight's oeuvre with the ac-
companiment of Monk's music. (Imagine "Misterioso" behind "The
Idea of Ancestry.") It helps to *hear* what was on the line for Knight.
I hazard the guess that the poet would have also asked, with Monk:
"What's all this stuff about 'race' and 'Negroes' you writing, man?"

::

Knight is dead—little rewarded, almost invisible among even a hip,
young, Nelly-influenced generation of black critics who think they

know something. But still, I hazard another guess. Knight would have said to me (in our hypothetical kick-back, jazz-listening session) something like: "Beware of Negroes bringing parody, my brother. And watch out for those who ignore my Mississippi harmonics, thinking they're *outside* the cage just because they listen to Monk and they got a little change in their pockets." If nothing else, Knight was cryptically brilliant at making the unseen "a scene." I miss him, in this locked room, listening to the firm piano punches of Thelonious Sphere Monk in Philadelphia deep freeze. The CD repeats "Ruby, My Dear," which I am hearing again for the very first time.

::

It is Sunday morning in Durham, North Carolina. I have escaped the record lows of Philadelphia and the close spaces of the hotel. Alone at first light in my study, I crank up the mood with a combination of Freddie Hubbard, Jacques Derrida, and, of course, Thelonious Monk. I know this morning that my reflections on skin color, black speech, and white critical expectations need exemplification. I need a recent example of black experimental creativity. (Freddie Hubbard follows a funky combo of piano and drums into "One Mint Julep.") I need a present-day, witty, rambunctious, deftly intelligent work by an African American writer, one that utterly mocks, rebukes, and refuses even the conditions of possibility for a question such as: "Who speaks for the Negro?"

It is not entirely by happenstance that I select as my example the author Percival Everett and his novel *Erasure* (2001). I am always traveling. And I have been invited to a conference in South Carolina, where I am expected to speak on Everett. This Sunday morning, I have a job that allows me to follow Freddie Hubbard's trumpet, read Jacques Derrida, work entirely at home, *and* enhance my understanding of black literature and literary criticism by analyzing *Erasure*. I am blessed.

::

Erasure is but one recent addition to the multifaceted list of Percival Everett's literary creations. Everett has produced thirteen works of fiction. For *Erasure*, he received the inaugural Hurston/Wright Legacy Award for Fiction. He is a southerner by birth, having spent his formative years in Columbia, South Carolina. I have, thus, been assigned by the South Carolina conference to a sort of native son, an unplanned bit of irony (which will become apparent in due course) on the part of the conference organizers. In some measure, Everett is an academic novelist who has navigated posts at Notre Dame and the Universities of Wyoming, Kentucky, California at Riverside, and (currently) Southern California. He and his writing are, by turns, engagingly smart, difficult, allusive, subtle—and always rich in the resources of parody and satire. What better choice, then, could there be on this Lord's day than *Erasure*? After all, I certainly do not wish—despite its classical status—to reread *Invisible Man* for the thousandth time and enter it (yet again!) in the American academic parade as the *non plus ultra* of African American "experimentalism." Moreover, as we shall see, one cannot take up *Erasure* without encountering the annoyingly familiar ghost of Ralph Ellison. Everett's novel provides, therefore, a kind of two-for-one bonus.

⁝⁝

Erasure draws a bead and focuses satiric crosshairs on the genealogy, archive, and bibliography—the lock—of the cage of black cultural representation in America. It is, therefore, an X novel, where the "X" signals the extermination of all limitations on the speech, voice, and subject matter of any man, woman, or child in the United States who writes or aspires to be a writer. Thelonious Monk once said: "If you really understand the meaning of be-bop, you understand the meaning of freedom." Percival Everett is about the be-bop inscription of black American artistic freedom. And we know we are in for an uproarious, nontraditional ride from the outset of his novel. For some of the book's early sentences read: "My name is Thelonious Ellison. I am a writer of fiction. . . . call me Monk."

BANG!

Our critical sensibilities are immediately closed to dialect, black rural agrarianism, and funky urban ghetto blackness. For here, fictionally, is God's experimental and sophisticated plenty! Monk and Ellison, Melville ("Call me Ishmael") and Twain. *Erasure* is formally designed as a confession *d'outre tombe*: "Since however I will be dead, it should not matter to me who sees what or when," says the narrator. And the novel is graced by an epigraph from Twain (who wrote his own *d'outre tombe* narrative) that juxtaposes "truth" and "lying." We are, thus, situated with Thelonious "Monk" Ellison in the traditional and classic American literary grain. But the narrator of *Erasure* has not had much success—at least, not as an experimental, academic, creative writer. His books don't do well. They are utterly "unmarketable," despite the associations of the author's name with such geniuses of black creativity as Ralph Ellison and Thelonious Sphere Monk. Percival Everett's "Monk" is a woodworker and fly fisherman (with shades of Richard Brautigan's *Trout Fishing in America*). He is one of the ubiquitous English Department-creative-writing-marginal-figures who thinks he must be brilliant, multilingual, and prophetic *because* he is totally ignored. "Monk" acknowledges his unmarketable "invisibility"—but still believes he is licensed to "tell us ALL." Thelonious Ellison, in short, is talented, innovative, and a man of resentment. He holds only two truths to be self-evident. The first is that all American public life and institutions are marked by vulgar materialism and crass banality. Second (and in oddly sentimental manner), he endorses filial piety, accepting tender responsibility for the elder care of his mother and guardianship of the Ellisons' faithful household servant, Lorraine.

⠃⠃

At first blush, analyzing a novel like *Erasure* would not seem to require the heavy theoretical instrumentation of Jacques Derrida. But the critical work of the French philosopher will prove essential to our inquiry. Why? Well, because no matter how "colored" the name Thelonious Ellison sounds, we are, we remember (O, shades of James Weldon Johnson) analyzing an X novel.

From the title page onward, the text of *Erasure* is marked by Xs—across titles and chapter headings, as breaking graphics between sections of the work. These Xs are everywhere in *Erasure* because it is a philosophically situated work of art. Situated in *Western* philosophy, to be sure, but definitely philosophically situated. And in the Western philosophical tradition, from Nietzsche to Derrida, X is the mark signaling "under erasure" (in French: *sous rature*).

In the work of Nietzsche and Derrida, to place a word in a sentence under X is to place that word's conceptual status under suspicion. Does the word marked by the X have a clear meaning and direct relationship to the world? Does it come to us metaphysically ordained—accented, as it were, by God? "No," says Derrida. There is no metaphysical pathway leading outside, behind, or beyond "writing." "There is nothing," he says, "outside the text." And writing, conceived as text, is always *nonoriginal* (we are *born*, as it were, *inside* writing). Writing is slippery and elusive, refusing to allow us (with any metaphysical certainty) to choose any one meaning or mode of interpretation over another. "Deconstruction" is the name given to the antimetaphysical thought and practices of X-men such as Derrida and his followers.

(Monk looks quizzical but unbedazzled by the turns and twists of X. I imagine his simple reduction of it all to a question: "So, what you're saying is that *my* 'Ruby, My Dear' is always already *in* any 'Ruby, My Dear'—even though I know mine is the hippest, right? Just like Ray Charles's 'America' is not competing with any so-called original. Right?" "Something like that," is all I manage before he swings out on rhythms of "Bud Walked In.")

::

Erasure's narrator is a deconstructionist—an X-man—in practice and thought. He is so far inside the text of the world he inhabits that he is able (with brilliant cynicism) to bite the very (academic) hand that feeds him. For example, at the annual meeting of the Nouveau Roman Society for experimental critics and writers, Monk presents a satirical paper titled "F/V: Placing the Experimental Novel." The paper is a three-thousand-word analysis of a single sentence that reads: "There are said to be certain Buddhists whose ascetic practices enable them to see a whole landscape in a bean." The paper is a parody of the critic Roland Barthes's *S/Z*, a critically enshrined work whose footnoting and abstruse energies of poststructuralism render a theoretical account of Balzac's *Sarrasine*. When Thelonious Ellison concludes his talk, he has achieved his goal. His audience is furious. One of them hurls a set of keys at his head and shouts: "You bastard!" Monk is not fazed. He responds: "Listen, I'm sorry you didn't like the paper, but I believe you misunderstood something. I don't even think about you guys, much less write about you" (36).

"You guys"? Isn't Monk himself—experimental writer, member of the Nouveau Roman—one of those guys? Yes, he is. But I think we as readers may be expected (in the context of Everett's novel) to laugh *with* Monk. He is intended to be a sympathetic character. I am not certain we are supposed to recognize—even in a fictional and deconstructionist vein—the utter boorishness of his virtuosic theoretical display with "F/V."

Ironically, however, "F/V" demands so much insider knowledge of the critical jargon for its effects and pleasures that Everett's protagonist (unwittingly) seems but to add highfalutin deconstructionist insult to what he deems the pretentious poststructuralist injury—to aesthetic common sense—of his academic peers. My sense is that the ordinary reader might have a very difficult time empathizing with Monk as he proceeds, with creepy and solipsistic self-certainty, through the world—believing he alone is capable of placing the contemporary culture industry *sous rature*. Still, even if we cannot sympathize with Monk's personality, we dare not gainsay his redoubtable talents as a satirist. He is a lampooner of the first order. His parodies of American television's pop culture and quiz shows are masterpieces. His send-up of *Jeopardy* (titled *Virtue et Armis*), in particular, is stunning in its deconstruction and critique of the supposed allegiance between popular media's banal versions of truth and knowledge and anything even vaguely resembling real knowledge or intelligence.

Mr. Dullard, the white contestant on *Virtue et Armis*, is asked to name a primary color. "Green," says Mr. Dullard. He is incorrect. The host now turns to the black contestant: "Tom, what is 'anaphase'?" And Tom: "Anaphase is the phase of nuclear division characterized by the movement of chromosomes from the spindle equator to the spindle poles" (175). Tom is correct! Tom continues to be correct, while Dullard fails and fails and fails. Tom wins. The host is disappointed. "The [white studio] audience made no sounds. They were dead." The rhythm and meter of *Virtue et Armis* and the characters Monk brings to its stage are perfect. A satirical bull's-eye! *Erasure* offers equally hilarious send-ups of Oprah Winfrey's predilection for popular prurience (the *Kenya Dunston Show*), and casts piercingly satirical barbs at Jerry Springer, the American media's prime panderer to all that is worst in the human spirit (the *Snookie Crane Show*).

Kenya Dunston never tires of treating television audiences to her Mammy-as-rich-and-troubled-black-girlfriend camaraderie. And it is on her show that Monk first actually witnesses the burgeoning popularity of the black Juanita Mae Jenkins, author of the chart-climbing novel *We's Lives in the Ghetto*.

Monk happens upon *We's Lives in the Ghetto* in a commercial superstore, immediately after finding his own experimental novel—a refiguration of classical mythology—filed under "African American studies." He reflects: "I became quickly irate, my pulse speeding up, my brow furrowing. Someone interested in African American studies would have little interest in my books and would be confused by their presence in the [African American studies] section" (28). Why is Monk's work in the African American studies section? Because its dustjacket photograph pictures a black man. (Here, again, is the insidious correlation between skin color and the presumed character of one's experience and speech.) "*Who* speaks for the Negro?"

As Monk walks away from the shelf holding his books, he sees an advertisement for *We's Lives in the Ghetto*. He picks up a copy of the book and reads its first lines: "My fahvre be gone since time I's borned and it be just me an' my momma an' my baby brover Juneboy. In da mornin' Juneboy never do brushes his teefus, so I gots to remind him. Because dat, Momma says I be the 'sponsible one and tell me that I gots to holds things togever while she be at work clean dem white people's house" (28–29).

Monk is undone, disgusted, embarrassed. For him, *We's Lives in the Ghetto* is the fictional equivalent of "a display of watermelon-eating, banjo-playing darkie carvings and a pyramid of Mammy cookie jars" (29).

Yet the book's profits are far more exalted. It has fetched $3 million in movie rights. On the *Kenya Dunston Show*, Miss Jenkins—who was born and raised in Ohio—reveals she based her "Negro novel" on a two-day visit to relatives in Harlem. Hence, while it is representative of neither actual black experience nor actual black speech, Jenkins's book comes to the public eye as one more bona fide example of the real (black) thing. Does *she*, therefore, speak for the Negro?

A Drink with Monk

Monk is reported

> one evening, after the last tune of his set . . . [to have] leaped up from the bench, his hands held in the attitude he had assumed as he finished the number, and without changing the attitude [hands up and in front of him as he lifted them from the piano's keys], he wheeled off the stand and did a long drawn out shuffle step from the stand completely around to the back of the club . . . [came] to a stop right at the center of the bar . . . called to the bartender "Give me a drink."

Thelonious Sphere Monk had attitudes—a "Monk's mood" that did not require him to give wide berth to others. Others energetically made room for *him*. They craved him—like finely aged malt—making music in the very rooms they inhabited. I imagine Thelonious Sphere asking: "Why did that brother—you know, Everett—use *my* name if he can't just leave other folks' nonsense alone? He need to find *his own* shuffle step, relax and have a double bourbon." "Well," I respond, "there's something about brothers getting their noses out of joint at the high-priced success of black women writers. And if you think back to Nathaniel Hawthor——" "Yeah, yeah, yeah," he cuts me off. "Who does he think he is—Ishmael Reed?" I laugh.

::

Driven to distraction by his obsessive resentment of the popular success of a black woman author who has cunningly jerry-built her "black experience" and "black talk" while achieving paid glory, Monk determines to "out-Herod Herod." Cynically, he makes up his mind to (in the phrase of Ralph Ellison) "change the joke and slip the yoke"—to join the company of the famous and infamous American tricksters, masqueraders, and jokesters, those who wear the mask in order to undo forms and conditions under which they feel oppressed. (Ellison instances the Bostonian whites who masqueraded as Indians for the Boston Tea Party that signaled the first full stirrings of the American Revolution.) Monk seats himself at his dead father's desk in the family home in Washington, D.C. He drafts with lightning speed a raucous burlesque of Richard Wright's world-renowned and celebrated *Native Son.*

Published in 1940, *Native Son* established Wright as the racially truthful, authentic "voice of the Negro." Thelonious Ellison sees Wright and his novel as the anchor and source of the white critical expectations that hold the black experimentalist in bondage, locked in a cage of realism's making. Monk *hates* realism. He deplores, in fact, the single realistic novel he has written, disparagingly titled *Second Failure.* (And that novel sold!) He signals his contempt for Wright and his fiction with the title he chooses for his parody of *Native Son.* Monk calls his burlesque *My Pafology.*

A reader of *Erasure* might be inclined at this juncture to inquire of Everett's protagonist: "Why Wright? Why not Juanita Mae Jenkins as the fictional character who enrages you, the character? Are you looking simply to knock off all 'real' globally recognized black authors?" Such an interrogation of formal logic, however, would yield no fruit. Because the logic of Monk's parody of Wright lies outside the text of *Erasure.*

::

In effect, Everett's selection of Richard Wright and *Native Son* as texts for derision shares a genealogy with what critic Harold Bloom calls the "anxiety of influence." I shall take up this anxiety of influence in due course, but for the moment, I want to note that the odd structural logic of Monk's seemingly arbitrary choice of *Native Son* complements the other strained structural logics of *Erasure*, for example, the almost unbearably tedious main narrative line of the novel. *Erasure's* main storyline might well be titled *My Dysfunktion: The Death of a Black Bourgeois Family*. Why does Everett compel his readers to attend to an utterly predictable and tepidly told romance of a philandering father who commits suicide, a mother verging on Alzheimer's, a sister and brother who make hash of their marriages and vocations? There are so many novels that tell such tales—and do it so much better than *Erasure*. (Sue Miller comes to mind as an accomplished author of family sagas.) Everett's utterly commercial, vapidly conventional story of a dysfunctional family loosely binds *Erasure* together. The main track of the narrative is artistically unworthy and anomalous—strangely out of keeping with the arch fear and loathing of vulgar, materialistic, pop-culture pandering that characterizes Everett's protagonist. The main storyline, in fact, undercuts Monk in quite odd ways, transforming a deconstructive antinomian author into a fly-fishing worker, an academic "good son." This pious sibling sells his beloved California residence and moves back to the family home to care for his aging mother. The principal storyline of *Erasure* is wispy sugar-coated sappiness. Everett's Monk transports Mahler and memories of summering on the Chesapeake to the retirement community where his mother is dying with Alzheimer's. Mother and son sharing chords (and cords) of sweet family death. And it is against the backdrop of such conventionality that we are asked to read Monk's parody of the world-famous Richard Wright as an act of a creative genius?! Cognitive dissonance is in full effect.

The protagonist of Thelonious Ellison's burlesque *My Pafology* is named Van Go, and what a piece of work he is! He is the father of four babies by four different black women. His vocabulary is replete with obscenity. He is a sociopath. When offered an opportunity to work for a rich black man named Mr. Dalton, Van Go rapes Dalton's daughter, Penelope. The following morning, he appears on the *Snookie Crane Show*, where he is confronted by the mothers of his babies.

There follow: murder, a car chase, and the televised police capture of
Van Go. (O, shades of poor O. J. Simpson!) THE END.

Ellison signs his manuscript "Stack R. Leigh," donning the mask
he deems most fitting for his artistic rebellion against black realism.
Monk thus plays in and on the field of the black vernacular, for, of
course, "Stackalee" is one of the most famous black bad-man bal-
lads in the Afro-American folk tradition. It is the story of a gam-
bler who shoots his best friend and goes straight to hell (as one of
the epigraphs of the present chapter recounts). Monk dispatches his
product to his agent, Yul.

In tribute to *Erasure*'s best satirical energies, *My Pafology* (later re-
titled simply *FUCK*) is a wickedly energetic and occasionally humor-
ous parody of African American writing that advertises itself as the
authentic speech of "the Negro." It profits accordingly. The parody
occupies fully a quarter of *Erasure*. It is, one might say, the voluminous and chastising BIG X (and hex) on Wright and realism. It is a
clever novel within a novel that fully enables *Erasure*'s ensuing plot
twists. The fate of *My Pafology/FUCK* serves as comic, deprecating critique of Thelonious Ellison's creative enterprise. And the structure
of Everett's novel as a whole seems almost to hold.

⁚⁚

I traveled to South Carolina (portable CD player and Thelonious
Monk disks in hand) and presented my findings, anxious to hear
what my almost completely white audience (there were two black
people present) had to offer. To a person, they hated *Erasure*'s main
storyline of family dissolution, skipped or glossed the sidebars from
Barthes to *Virtue et Armis*, did not know what to make of Kenya Dunston, but . . . adored, and could quote almost by the paragraph, *My
Pafology/FUCK*.

Thus, college professors at the conference by the Beaufort River
averred that what their classes loved most about *Erasure* was *My Pafology*. Retired white professionals wistfully cited *My Pafology*'s ungainly
prose as "the best part of the novel." Were they all suffering from too
much Oprah and Jerry Springer, and too little Wright? Perhaps. But
what seems more likely is that *My Pafology*'s ugly transformation of

a complicated black fiction and fictional character (*Native Son* and Bigger Thomas) into simple blackface, urban darkie "jokeology" and deep minstrel stereotype produces the palatable "who speaks for the Negro?" appeal of the one-quarter of *Erasure* my South Carolina audience voted its top pick. The transfiguration worked by *My Pafology* on Richard Wright's realism might be called the alchemy of successful authorial blackface in America.

It is always popular in America to derogate the life of the black American majority, through "thugcraft" trappings and Mammy cookie jars. Scandalizing the word "Negro" sells in America, and it sells well. It goes over just great with white audiences. The conference folks in South Carolina, obviously, were no exception. The structure of *Erasure* that actually held their attention was the brute nonsense of minstrelsy—*Erasure*'s own tribute to and ironic comradeship with Jerry, Oprah, and Alex Trebek.

::

Stack R. Leigh, the pseudonym and signature Thelonious Ellison uses for *My Pafology*, is merely a citation—not a real person, much less an authentic black author. The signature is only a sign of authorship. But, presumably, because a popular art world, television establishment, and motion picture moguldom are so lost in the metaphysics of a definite-articled Negro (albeit thugged- and minstreled-up), they buy *My Pafology* as the real thing. (Alas, my South Carolina audience, then, stepped right in line with the racist, corporatist, pop-cultural basement of American entertainment.) To our protagonist Monk's aesthetic horror—but capitalist pleasure—his parody of Richard Wright garners huge critical, commercial, and popular success. To paraphrase a Victorian classic: "He is Juanita Mae Jenkins, and she is he!"

Monk's spoof receives an advance of $600,000; movie rights come in at $3 million. Book club adoption doubles the advance. And the white popular entertainment corporate complex simply cannot get enough of ol' Stack R. Leigh and his Negro novel. Even though the author's very name belies what, essentially, is a joke! Sure, Monk is black, but he "can't play basketball; can't dance; doesn't believe in 'race'" (133).

Much in the manner of Ralph Ellison's character Rinehart (rind/ heart) from *Invisible Man,* Monk wears a "mask" that enables him to shape-shift, shift registers. Behind the mask, he can become commercially mobile while hiding, or confess his guilt or innocence at will. For Ralph Ellison, as already noted, this mask is the quintessential put-on of American national identity. "America," says Ellison, "is a land of masking jokers. We wear the mask for purposes of aggression as well as defense" (*Invisible Man,* 70).

Monk Bids Adieu

In 1973, Monk vanished from the Big Apple—the Vanguard, the Blue Note, and all that jazz. He moved into the Weehawken, New Jersey, house of the Baroness Nica de Koenigswarter. She said: "He's withdrawn, that's all. It's as though he has gone into retreat." Did Monk don a mask of silence? He did not touch a piano after 1976. The character Michel-Jean Scélérat in Orlando Lima's fine first novel, *No Room for Squares,* says of Monk's retreat: "People loved his music, but no one understood the language he was creatin' it with. How could they? He was masterin' calculus while everybody else was flunkin' subtraction" (138). Black genius distancing itself from the throes of American minstrel expectations? The tragedies of anxiety? Who has the last laugh? Can I, writing today in the overcast of a North Carolina Sunday morning, legitimately digitally remaster a dancing Monk back into my parentheses in self-defense? The "Blue Monk" coolly swings into play, sounding for the world like inverse Ellington. Outside is in and vice Monk-style versa. After Stack R. Leigh and his authoring of the obscenity *FUCK* have made him the beloved black of the entertainment corporatist complex, Everett's Monk says:

> I wondered how far I should take my Stagg [*sic*] Leigh performance. I might in fact become a Rhinehart [*sic*], walking down the street and finding myself in store windows. I yam

what I yam. I could throw on a fake beard and a wig and do the talk shows, play the game, walk the walk, shoot the jive. No, I couldn't.

I would let Mr. Leigh continue his reclusive, just-out-of-the-big-house ways. He would talk to the editor a few more times, then disappear, like down a hole. (162)

Genius can say adieu and mean it. But can intellectual meanness really hide?

::

Alas, neither Stack nor the annoying philosophical meanderings of Thelonious Ellison do disappear. (Which is to say, *Erasure*'s partial failure is that of an exorbitant one-trick pony—a weak storyline spangled by stunning sidebars.) In fact, *FUCK* wins everything. The annual televised Book Award goes to Monk. It is a corporate affair as the protagonist notes: "I was seated with . . . the CEO of General Mills, a vice president from General Motors, and head of marketing for General Electric" (262). We see the subtraction of the sellout in the following words:

> So, I would not be economically oppressed because of writing a book that fell in line with the very books I deemed racist. And I would have to wear the mask of the person I was expected to be. I had already talked on the phone with my editor as the infamous Stagg Leigh and now I would meet with Wiley Morganstein [a movie mogul]. I could do it. The game was becoming fun. And it was nice to get a check. (212)

Finally, then, for all the aesthetic posturing and moral meditation of Thelonious Ellison, we have a cryptically sleazy commercialism as the triumphant norm: "Call it expediently located irony, or convenient rationalization, but I was keeping the money" (260). Thus, the anxiety of influence morphs not into deconstructive and aesthetically radical rebellion or erasure, but into a kind of mad exhausted submission and the exuberance of getting paid. The talented and successful present-day rapper Nelly captures this economics of compromise in a single line: "Must be the money!"

❖

Who speaks for the Negro? Percival Everett and his engaging protagonist in *Erasure* lead us once again to the question. They kick off the critical set for revisiting the inquiry. They drive us back through a genealogy and critical history of influence and reception. And the answer to the question offered by *Erasure* seems to be that no (black) one speaks or can speak for the Negro. The *who* would seem rather (and still) to be an empowered elite of the white culture industry, motivated by what we might call "burnt-cork envy." They know what they wish to hear as "Negro." They want, like good old Norman Mailer's man of desire, *The White Negro*, to judge and to be him.

For example, the white television producer, Dunwitty (so magnificently played by Michael Rapaport), in Spike Lee's film *Bamboozled*, tells his African American script writer: "I am *blacker* than you are." Dunwitty is, I think, a latter-day version of those enduring southern fugitives of America. They are the white guys who get to choose and determine what is truly "Negro" or "black" for America's intellectual and entertainment industrial complex. And this complex always demands the definite article.

Percival Everett and *Erasure* are energetically aware of this intellectual and entertainment industrial complex, and strive, in powerful antimetaphysical ways, to escape its enervating reductions of black life and culture. Yet the structural course of *Erasure* and its protagonist, Thelonious, is deeply problematic: saccharine main storyline; one-quarter of the text devoted to, alas, a minstrel reduction of Richard Wright; complicit resignation to an aesthetics of capital success; and a not-so-subtle leitmotif of class warfare and resentment toward both the black ghetto majority and the old and nouveau black bourgeoisie (cf. the black Mr. Dalton as ambulance-chasing attorney, and his expensively educated daughter, the pothead Penelope).

Reviewers and pedagogues alike have dubbed *Erasure* a satirical, antimetaphysical, wittily original manifestation of racially transcendent creativity that successfully unlocks the cage of "Negro speaking." And surely the novel *is* original, even if Ishmael Reed's "talking [black] androids" of *Mumbo Jumbo* and *The Last Days of Louisiana Red* are clear predecessors to Van Go. Yet I find myself unpersuaded. I do not find *Erasure* (replete as it is with masculinist bravado and tongue-in-cheek anti-black-majority sentiment) to contain the redeeming grace notes proclaimed by reviewers.

In part, I know my resistance to such critical kudos has to do with my travels—and the insistent voice and music of Thelonious Monk that has been so instructive to my inquiry.

::

I throw *The Best of Thelonious Monk* into the CD player in my study on this subzero Tuesday in what I am told is the "sunny South." Ha! I follow the rhythmic punches of Monk's fingers, which I imagine parallel to the keys; I think about the question *who speaks for the Negro?* and what role *Erasure* plays in the economies of this inquiry. My first thought: "You *have* to talk," I say to no one in particular or, maybe, to Monk: "You have to talk more about Richard Wright." "Misterioso" is playing—against the cold—and memory tells me I did promise to come back to the "anxiety of influence."

Richard Wright's collection of short stories titled *Uncle Tom's Children* (1938), his novel *Native Son* (1940), and his autobiography, *Black Boy* (1945), constitute one of the most antimetaphysical trilogies of writing in the white American and African American literary canons. I do not wish to debate this proposition here—there is on record already a rich abundance of discussion on this matter. The reader who has traveled this far with me is free to look to the works of theorists, critics, novelists, and reviewers who have affirmed or contested this proposition. What I instance, therefore, is not debate but what I shall call the "evidence of anxiety."

Insubstantial or featherweight triumphs of imagination become either entirely forgotten or, at best, minor literatures. Richard Wright's achievements are, by contrast, *classic* and *classical.* Their standing may change as values and evaluation shift. But today, in 2007, Wright is classic material. And it is certain that a genealogy of

African American writers since the 1940s has been nearly apoplectic with anxiety over the Mississippi black boy (not unlike Etheridge Knight) and his success in avoiding silence and holding onto an indisputable global renown. James Baldwin had to meet this anxiety of influence head-on, up-close and personal with the very Richard Wright who mentored him and secured for him a fellowship to Paris to finish his first novel. The influential critic Harold Bloom argues, according to one of his admirers:

> The primary struggle of the young poet [such as Baldwin] is against the old masters. He, the ephebe, must "clear imaginative space" for himself through a creative misreading of the strong poets of the past. Only strong poets can overcome this anxiety of influence; lesser lights become derivative flatterers and never achieve poetic immortality for themselves.

Richard Wright's role in this Bloomian drama is clearly that of the "strong poet." Baldwin's struggle with Wright took the form of merciless attacks on what he labeled the "protest novel," tracing its history from Harriet Beecher Stowe's *Uncle Tom's Cabin* to Wright's *Native Son*. In a word, Baldwin felt such novels—black realism, as it were—were incapable of "racial truth," because they never escaped the social arena of stock writing and a sentimental theology of good and evil. Protest novels were morally and ethically shallow rituals for exorcising black sin and evil. Still, in mid-career, Baldwin produced his bestselling fiction, *Another Country*, in which he adheres, with sometimes awkward fidelity, to the structural principles and morals that he defines as characteristic of, precisely, the protest novel.

Ralph Ellison, whose first job as writer and first mentoring in the writer's vocation were at the hands of Richard Wright, found it necessary to repudiate the author of *Native Son* in some of his most modishly "nonracial" prose. He writes, for example, in his famous essay "The World and the Jug":

> I have no objections to being placed beside Richard Wright in any estimation which is based not upon the irremediable

ground of our common racial identity, but upon the quality
of our achievements as writers. I respected Wright's work
and I knew him, but this is not to say that he "influenced"
me as significantly as you [the white critic Irving Howe] assume. . . . as early as 1940 Wright viewed me as a potential
rival, partially, it is true, because he feared I would allow
myself to be used against him by political manipulators
who were not Negro and who envied him.

Truth is, I think that Wright is unequivocally the "strong poet."
And what makes him so is his implacable resolve to go to the material, oligarchic, fascist, hurtful, powerful, and detrimental realities
and agents of America's lockdown and confinement of blacks . . . to
make his way precisely to the ghetto and its corporately mandated
and controlled ghetto obscenity. Wright knew such obscenity had its
defining origins in the economies of the plantations of the so-called
New World, in the type of economics that had been his own first residence, and that had spread racism, greed, brutality, and, ultimately,
secession and murderous civil warfare across a continent. The wake
of the Civil War brought a northern capitalist train of consequences,
accompanied by lynching and Jim Crow. Wright went global, as it
were, on the awful American economies of color and capital.

Wright was unafraid to explain, precisely—and yes, it is still
true—that, for the most part and in the majority, we (black people/
Negroes) do, in fact, "lives in the ghetto." This is an uncomfortable
and anxiety-producing reality, to be sure, but not one we can ac-
cuse Richard Wright of having created. Nor can we ignore the fact
that he produced fictional classics that still offer resonant takes on
this reality. Wright's call to black authors (see "Blueprint for Negro
Writing") was to get at the truth of "the way we live now," and to relinquish comprador-like seductions of white audiences that render
clever bourgeois portrayals of black respectability as the "truth" of
our majority lives.

██
██

Thelonious (Monk) Ellison, protagonist of *Erasure*, devotes a good deal of witty artistic energy to asides and cameos that feature post–World War I European expressionist artists. The expressionists, such as Barlach, Klee, Kollwitz, Mueller, and Dix, pledged their lives and work to exposé and opposition. They went head-on against the militaristic German Right and its rich, conservative sponsors. They were aesthetic revolutionaries, facing down oppression, corruption, totalitarianism. Many of them suffered the consequences: exile, imprisonment, and death. This attention to these post–World War I expressionists in *Erasure* would seem to suggest, at least, a tacit endorsement of their artistic practice as a desirable politics of art. Of course, de Kooning's abstract expressionism and Rauschenberg's eclectic life and aesthetic proclivities—his taste for outsiders, which brought him scorn from the New York art elite—these are artistically rebellious and against-the-grain creativities that would scarcely revert to bourgeois, sentimental genre prints. However, *Erasure* itself offers no emulation, replication, or even a hint that its author, or the narrator, is prepared to offer up such contestatory politics of art, or to engage in such a dangerous project as an actual political resistance.

No, *Erasure*, for all its parodic and deconstructive energy and achievement is completely clean, clear, and empty before what I believe is the signal social and political fact of its time, namely, the Ronald Reagan/George Herbert Walker Bush compromise of American decency and rights that has produced George W. Bush, the son and heir of indecency, and his jack-booted ideology and train of mercenary fellows in the White House. The crew behind the invasion of Iraq and the neglect and horror that marked the federal response to Hurricane Katrina. Where is the contestation or parody or *je refuse!* of *Erasure* with respect to the historical and ongoing ignominy of its time and place in the literary world?

Erasure's narrator wallows in the anguish of anxiety before the success of Richard Wright (and, not incidentally, that of black women writers in the United States). But he never lives up to the against-the-grain artistic ideals he so delights in dazzling before readers as sidebars.

Still, there is virtue in the life and work of Thelonious Ellison and his creator, Percival Everett. *Erasure* does compel us to summon the actual Monk—Thelonious Sphere Monk—and his music, his achievement. And, as importantly, reading the novel drives us back to Richard Wright and forces a deconstruction, in our own imperiled time, of the dread undertow and corporately maintained entailments of the seemingly simple query: "Who speaks for the Negro?" These are good outcomes of *Erasure*, and we must be thankful for them.

::

(The sun is setting over North Carolina ice and snow. Monk nods, winks at me, and says: "I was never in hiding, man. There was just no one to play for." He seems pleased to have helped me flush the white and black conservative covey on the question "Who speaks for the Negro?" I think, on this frigid evening, how sumptuous a double bourbon would be—with Monk, and Knight . . . straight no chaser.)

Failed Prophet and Falling Stock

Why Ralph Ellison Was Never Avant-Garde

> If history were the past, history wouldn't matter.
> History is the present, the present. You and I are history.
>
> —James Baldwin, *a rap on race*

N ow, of course, it was long before the days of Ralph Ellison that
artistic Negroes got the notion they could be sufficiently liberated by white critics to be judged by standards other than whether
they actually spoke for *the* Negro. Phillis Wheatley let her audience
hear her eulogies in Latinate classically allusive tones, even as she
assured them that Negroes "black as Cain" may be baptized and join
the (white) angelic train. Ol' Fred Douglass eventually got his oratory pumped so high, and his super-American (dare one say, imperialist) patriotism so revved, that one might have listened from white
to black and not been able to tell the difference. To where did all the
rich, liberating vernacular idiom and impulse of Douglass's 1845 *Narrative of the Life of Frederick Douglass* recede? By the 1920s, an intellectually
anxious Melvin Tolson was bent on creating high-modern allusive

poetical epics that not even Robert Penn Warren could mistake for the voice of *the* Negro.

No, Ellison, like the 1920s Negro poet Countee Cullen, is only part of a long line of black men and women who have wanted to be judged by a standard other than the "irremediable ground of . . . a common racial identity." Legions have made the bid to escape critical scrutiny as "Negro writers," desiring mightily to be "just writers." As with the product that is *Erasure*, many of the efforts of the Legion of Just Writers have been captivating. They have taken us a bit higher, expanded the cell dimensions and incarcerating amenities of the cage of black writing in America just a bit. Yet what has so often been inadequately accounted—ignored, distorted, misunderstood, or lost—in the legion's anxieties of influence has been the power of the black vernacular, the interests of the black majority, and the furtherance of the emancipatory tradition of black expressive culture in the Americas. Though he is far from first, chronologically, in this legion of the lost, Ralph Ellison represents the most spectacularly brilliant and influential failure of imagination of black writing in the Untied States. His novel *Invisible Man* is the *Hindenburg* of that fraught black American striving to be *just a* (no prefix needed) *writer*. Ellison's is the most spectacular craft ever to fly under the expectations and anxieties of a race-transcendent (read: white) judgment. His flight is, thus, signal, single, and spectacular. Percival Everett finds Ellisonian aviation so remarkable that he names his protagonist "Ellison." And now that we have our critical landing lights focused on black experimental expression, what more appropriate time could there be to examine the soaring failure of *Invisible Man* and its author with respect to the black vernacular—the interests, craft, and creativity of the black majority?

::

In later years of his career, a charge frequently leveled against Richard Wright was that he was old-fashioned, out of date, and clinging (even in content and style) to the memory of a Jim Crow ethics that critics insisted had passed from the American scene forever. In a sense, this charge of datedness implies that memory—and particularly a "racial" memory—forestalls modernity. What I would suggest is that Wright's astute awareness of the interconnections among race, power, economics, urbanity, and technology in the United States (an understanding conditioned by his southern racial memory and his own brand of Marxist analysis) enabled him to join a company of thinkers intent on achieving an empowering black global modernity. Hence, Wright cannot simply be viewed as a black person who was hurt, outraged, and terrified by U.S. racism. He must be understood as a courageous black intellectual informed by racial wisdom acquired during a life under the aegis of southern Jim Crow, and northern redlining and racist political assault. From the vantage of our new millennium moment, it seems ironic that the black intellectuals promoted to displace Wright during the 1950s were likable men. They commanded more conventional literary elegance than Wright. But they were also strikingly parochial in their understanding, representation, and relationship to southern, black American life. Of the novelist Ralph Ellison's relationship to the South, the black political scientist Jerry Gafio Watts in his monograph *Heroism and the Black Intellectual* writes:

> When reading Ellison's perceptions of the South one must remember that he did not experience the South from the vantage point of a native black southerner. Ellison's sense of possibility was decidedly that of a black raised outside the Deep South. . . . Ellison only experienced the periphery of southern black life during the age of Jim Crow. . . . Who but Ellison would have argued that attendance at a southern black college, life in a college town, and journeys to the countryside with the Tuskegee band would substantively immerse him in black life in the Deep South? (p. 86)

Of the black essayist James Baldwin's journey of self-discovery and activism to the American South, the critic Daryl C. Dance in her article "You Can't Go Home Again" observes: "His trip South so unnerved Baldwin that when he returned to New York, he collapsed, evidently suffering neurasthenia, or what he described as a paralysis resulting from retrospective terror" (p. 87). The irony of Wright's American displacement is heightened, I think, if we acknowledge that neither Ralph Ellison nor James Baldwin possessed a fraction of Wright's intelligence with respect to the dynamics of the unfolding world of postcolonial colored people.

Black modernity as elegant formalism is a panorama altogether different, I believe, from such modernity conceived in terms of a black critical memory that refuses to relinquish its racial roots. I believe critical memory compels the black intellectual such as Wright to keep before his eyes and the eyes of the United States a history that is embarrassing, macabre, and always bizarre with respect to race. The clarity bestowed by black critical memory is painful. It is a terrible lucidity, casting dark light on a deeply troubling racial idea. *Idea* is the proper word here. For, at least in the U.S., race always has more to do with a nest of images, fears, envies, fantasies, and anxieties than with the root life or everyday comings and goings of real people. However, this does not mean race is no more today than a burst of sound from intense social scientists. Race, alas, is still the ruling idea that conjures and pronounces sentences of guilt or innocence, life or death, acceptance or denial on we who are black by choice—or due to inescapable circumstance.

Now perhaps what is most disturbing about Ralph Ellison's displacement of Richard Wright in American economies of race, modernity, and taste is Ellison's utter failure as a prophet of tomorrow. For, in his single completed novel, Ralph Ellison missed altogether the revolutionary possibilities of black life in America as they unfolded, even while his book was in page proofs. Black revolutionary possibilities for black modernity became American realities even while a conservative Ralph Ellison seemed unable to make his narrative way beyond Trueblood and Bledsoe, missionary Christianity and incipient individualistic "slave rebellion"—a Brer Rabbit canniness of "black peasants" whose soiled likableness was genius to Booker T. Washington and George Washington Carver. Ellison's black South, unfortunately, does not transcend the Carver Museum at Tuskegee.

In the early 1950s, as we all know, a black southern public sphere was emerging that would lead to a cataclysmic rights revolution, altering the very course of U.S. history, influencing movements for liberation the world over. Dr. Martin Luther King, Jr., Rosa Parks,

Fannie Lou Hamer, Ella Baker, John Lewis, Autherine Lucy, legions of black youngsters on a "children's crusade," blacks and whites staffing a Freedom Summer against southern terror—these emergent agents of American rights were inconceivable to the author of *Invisible Man.* Or, at least, there is no hint of their imminence in *Invisible Man.* The grassroots resistance and organization—the utter determination for "freedom now"—that was bedrock for the Civil Rights movement in America make no appearance in *Invisible Man.* The novel provides only an accommodationist black populace brokered by the likes of Dr. Bledsoe into rank submissiveness before white trustees.

And when *Invisible Man* directs its attention to the North, it is scarcely more prophetic. Which is not to say there are no rebellious hipsters, hustling cartmen named Wheatstraw, and bodacious chameleon Rineharts in Ellison's northern imaginary. No, it is not that Ellison missed the futuristic black "underground" altogether. He simply failed, or refused, to inscribe the process of that underground transforming itself into a field of revolutionary energy that changed the ways of black American folk for all time.

What accounts for such silence? Why does Ellison fail to praise, champion, or flesh out the revolutionary potential of a black civil rights public sphere in the South, or to strongly portray a genuinely efficacious public field of Black Power advocacy in the North?

Fundamentally, I think Ellison's politics of silence with respect to these black public domains is, first, a product of his decision to hibernate during the harrowing days of McCarthyism. He was not comfortable or secure enough to run against the American grain during an age of blacklisting, deportation, and House Un-American Activities Committee interrogations. When the inquisition is in full effect, it may be better to play a bear (rather than a lion) in winter. Second, I believe Ellison sincerely believed in the ideals ardently preached by American business: ideals of industrial democracy as be-all and end-all of global modernity.

Modern humanity, for Ellison, is humanity attuned to the rhythms of the machine, to the currents and undercurrents of a raceless industrial capitalism. Modern humanity speaks and listens on an exclusively urban frequency, ever aware of ideological fault lines and complexities that make "social responsibility" a vexed obligation in a newly bureaucratic state. Hence, Ellison, I think, shares the politics and vision of an imperialist modernity, one of American exceptionalism. There is no trace in *Invisible Man*, for example, of global competition. In keeping with the Cold War mania of his era, however, there are certainly hints in *Invisible Man* of a pesky pinko outside agitation with respect to the Brotherhood's circuits of influence. Ellison seems utterly convinced that American modernity will—in part, presumably, through the philosophical musings of unengaged, hibernating, First Amendment black "thinker tinkers"—pull itself onto the raft of equal rights and stop lynching (literally and symbolically) black folks before another century has passed. Professor Jerry Watts, whom I have already cited, writes of Ellison's faith in industrial-democratic individualism and its resultant political and artistic consequences:

> During the past twenty (and perhaps thirty) years [since 1964], Ellison has not publicly been part of any organized black intellectual effort to confront racist practices in American intellectual life. Other black intellectuals have asked him to use his enormous prestige in this effort, but to no avail. . . . Ellison did not physically relocate to another land [like Baldwin or Wright], but his disengaged intellectual style may have been a necessary form of psychological immigration from the overbearing commitments and physiological demands that accompany a politically engaged black intellectual existence in America. Ellison's willingness and ability to create a world of healthy black adaptation to subjugation may be nothing less than an attempt to fashion an image of the world that morally legitimates his political disengagement. It is, perhaps, a guilt-reducing fiction. (pp. 111, 113)

In some ways, the fictional naïveté of Ellison's protagonist is completely emblematic of what might be called the presentist simplicity of *Invisible Man*'s own endorsement of industrial, imperialist, xenophobic American mythmaking. Layer upon layer upon layer of allusion mark *Invisible Man*'s chapters. In combination with the novel's veritably Homeric ambitiousness, these allusive layers serve finally to obscure rather than to prophesy the actual, engaged, advance-guard, public sphere effectiveness of American blacks already at work, bringing real inklings of democratic modernity to the United States.

Simply stated, Ellison believed morality, equality, and responsibility were affirmative "notions." And so they are. But blacks, at the very moment of *Invisible Man*'s receipt of literary awards on startling occasions, were transforming notions into decisively affirmative *action*—converting the shadow to the act of black liberation itself. A black majority was courageously putting body and soul on the line and constructing a sphere of American ethical publicity undreamed (or even subtly implied) by Ellison's promising American fictions. The black New York novelist was stonily silent on the possibilities of an altogether exceptional America—a postindustrial, radically black-public-sphere-conditioned America (or, better, Americas). He was no prophet, and where the black public sphere is concerned, *Invisible Man* provides no greatly prophetic matter.

Ellison's novel is burdened by belief, overwhelmed by excessive literary smartness, afraid to breathe life into its potentially revolutionary cartoons. For that, finally, is what so many figures on Ellison's fictional landscape are: mere cartoons, ventriloquized in the name of a certain species of democratic eloquence. They carry no black agentive weight that might threaten anything or anybody constituting—to quote Du Bois—the "best white public opinion" in America. But, surely, since Ralph Waldo Ellison has influenced the intellectual strivings of so many American liberal spokespeople, the foregoing assessment of *Invisible Man* must seem like dark, heretical ingratitude. But I mean no disrespect. I do mean, however, to honor my explicit claim to honest writing. Such critical judgments as I have made must be supported by the novel's own weight of evidence. Hence, a critical reading is in order to support my critique.

Where industry and its white captains are concerned, need we look further than the trustee Mr. Norton or the export mogul Mr. Emerson? On power as the product—both beneficent and terrible—of industrial machines, need we search beyond that southern campus road in *Invisible Man* "with its sloping and turning"? On this road is the "black powerhouse with its engines droning earth-shaking rhythms in the dark, its windows red from the glow of the furnace" (34). This uncanny scene of industrial power's dominance over black life reprises in the "deep basement" of Lucius Brockway at the northern Liberty Paint Factory. Here, machinery, furnaces, gauges lead the protagonist to an earth-shaking encounter with mysteries of American industry and industrialists alike. The hero's awe is palpable: "It's tremendous. It [Liberty Paint] looks like a small city," he exclaims (197). And in this "small city," he undergoes a machine-tooled rebirth from an electronic gizmo that subjects him to an industrial lobotomy (233, 243). The vagaries of black American life in the North come to seem like one huge industrial accident. Any benefits of industry that trickle down to blacks seem like pure products of welfare capitalism at its American worst. Which is to say, the benefits that supposedly accrued to blacks in the northern promised land—scandalously dirty and dangerous jobs in industrial plants, menial janitorial labor, domestic in-house peonage for black women, and death-dealing attendance on steel furnaces in, say, industrial Pittsburgh—were chimeras. The naïveté of Ellison's narrator—the impulse that leads him to believe Mr. Norton might be his savior—is nowhere more in evidence than in his miscalculations with respect to the "benefits" (health and otherwise) of northern industry.

Ellison's narrator—despite his use and abuse by both democracy and industry—seems to try desperately to hold on to a firm faith in industrial democracy. I think this is, in part, a function of *Invisible Man*'s anxious dependence on the brilliant analysis of the transition of black America from folk consciousness to an idealized industrial, participatory democracy that appears in Richard Wright's *12 Million Black Voices*. While it may be true that Ellison repudiated Wright as a literary ancestor, *Invisible Man*'s strong anxiety of influence seems, in our era, rather obvious. There simply is no insight with respect to black folk consciousness, black northern migration, or black urban/industrial existence in *Invisible Man* that is not anticipated by Wright's masterpiece *12 Million Black Voices*. Listen to Wright: "in industry . . . we encounter experiences that tend to break down the structure of our folk characters and project us toward the vortex of modern urban life."

Wright's narrative, however, understands that black factory work is merely a way to counter white labor union initiatives. It is always contingent upon a power politics of racial exclusion. Though blacks may work cheaply for Western civilization, says Wright, they are never allowed to live equally as citizens within Western civilization. Nevertheless, the Great Depression showed black and white workers their common class interests. The old black folk consciousness died an economically motivated death during the Great Depression. A beleaguered proletariat transcended barriers of race and class. The "bosses of the buildings" trembled before a new communalism, if not an actual progressive communism. Modernity, therefore, for Wright—a Wright whose politics are completely alien to Ellison's philosophizing hibernation—is nonfolk, industrial, and interracially proletarian.

Indeed, for Wright, modernity is at its best when it is engaged in strict scientific scrutiny and critique of capitalism and its bosses. Ellison's *Invisible Man* co-opts most of Wright's brilliant, poetic insights about black modernity. But Ellison cartoonizes a flesh-and-blood black majority's everyday life, as well as Wright's critique of capital. The author of *Invisible Man* pays little studied attention to the intimate horrors of racism in the United States. He relinquishes such analysis for a mess of Eliotian or Hemingwayesque allusions. Wright works as an embattled, public, activist, black intellectual. Ellison writes as though intellect is both color-blind and capable of effective, nonengaged, philosophical intervention in the terrors of race in these United States.

What locks Ellison so dramatically into a "color-blind," literarily allusive prison house of language is, I think, his novel's supposition that white policing and surveillance are utterly inescapable by black Americans. All black life in the United States, *Invisible Man* implies, is no more than a black battle royal. I refer, of course, to the scene in the novel in which the protagonist believes he is going to deliver an inspiring valedictory address to a group of influential white men at a posh hotel. Instead he is hurried, bare-chested, onto an elevator with a group of black young men; all have been fitted out with boxing gloves. When they arrive at the appointed hotel ballroom, instead of a podium, there is a boxing ring! The boys are forced to

fight—blindfolded—until there is only a "last man standing." It is
not the protagonist who is left standing; he is a bloodied victim of
the battle royal. But, the white men still invite him to speak for the
Negro. The scene suggests that black "territory" in America is no
more than a zone of containment without remedy, and impervious
to critique. White men set in motion black internecine warfare and
competition, degrade the economic necessities of the black world,
and then still want to be entertained by "Negro speaking"—of a
prescribed sort.

Here is Ellison's protagonist on being led into the hotel ballroom
for his first encounter with white discipline and punishment: "I was
shocked to see some of the most important men of the town quite
tipsy. They were all there—bankers, lawyers, judges, doctors, fire
chiefs, teachers, merchants. Even one of the more fashionable pas-
tors" (18). Of course, the protagonist's ironic "shock" is heightened
because he is the smartest (black) kid in his class. Even the valedictory
blacks, Ellison implies, can't escape the professional white gaze. The
protagonist believes he is being ushered into the ballroom to present, yet again, his high school valedictory address. After he is beaten
severely by one of his own, he still stands bloody but unbowed in
his American faith. He delivers his speech. It is about blacks staying
faithfully in their containment areas. When he stumbles upon the
phrase "social equality," he quickly retracts it under the immediate
threat of white professionalism. The invisible man is no native intellectual (read: organic intellectual). He is, rather, the "native" as
intellectual—ersatz intellectual, that is, in the service of white containment and clearance of black folks in America.

Like the factory and industrial power scene, this battle royal
leitmotif reprises in *Invisible Man*. Its politics of containment are apparent in the white American woman stripteaser who is brought in
by the "most important men of the town" to titillate white male
fantasy, and tempt bare-chested black boys. A voyeuristic white politics of body/sexual taboo and containment is contingent upon white
women's reduction to sex objects, and nothing more. Remember,
it is at the hero's most effective moment of Harlem Brotherhood
work that he is transferred from uptown to white downtown as an
all-but-bare-chested orator on the "woman question." He becomes a

black stud for white power. The sad politics of black men's and white women's disempowerment in America acquires a new convert.

Ralph Waldo Ellison—the valedictorian of Afro-American letters—reads the black public sphere as a labyrinthine scene of black men and (less frequently) women under the ideological power and powerful economic protocols of a white, male-dominated America. Ellison's reading (no matter how implicitly ironic) misses the nascent energy of civil rights and Black Power in the era in which he produced his one novel. And when civil rights and Black Power became American—indeed global—realities, Ellison reclined in butter-soft seats at exclusive Manhattan clubs, explaining to whites why he could not take any active part in the liberation politics of black Americans. America's industrial, democratic, lobotomizing machine—like the sleep of reason—had seemingly produced a club-able monster in a Ralph Ellison who could not be forgiven on the grounds that, like his fictional protagonist, he was just a young black man still in American citizenship formation. One is tempted to sample James Baldwin's postmortem of Richard Wright (without the ad hominem invective) and say: "Alas, poor Ralph!" He completely missed the real black modernity of America.

But this, of course, is not the entire picture. Ellison was obsessed with the power of a white, industrial, bureaucratic state (see Peter Wheatstraw's fetishizing of those ever-changing plans of the bosses of the buildings). His obsession forestalled effective prophecy for tomorrow, but it did not prevent his hearing around corners.

Invisible Man possesses a striking array of characters who make brief appearances, and then are seen no more are not those of idiots signifying nothing. Quite the contrary. These interlinear characters are precisely the ones Ellison's fear of McCarthyism—and an obsessive phobia of not being liked and well-off—kept him from fleshing out. The purveyors of possibilities of black, public, intellectual action I have in mind are Ras the Exhorter, Tod Clifton, Brother Tarp, Rinehart, Mary Rambo, and others. They are potentially activist and engaged Fanonian native intellectuals; they offer potential for effective black leadership in *Invisible Man*. They have broken manacles, dropped out of official history, learned the mastery of form, preserved and transformed the best of black folk consciousness, and are unbelievably eloquent. Brother Tarp is a model for Toni Morrison's Hi Man and Paul D in the stunning novel *Beloved.* Everywhere—interlinearly in *Invisible Man*—there simmers a potential for effective black public sphere leadership.

But the novel denies its own best insights by incarcerating all such potentially revolutionary figures in a Walt Disneyesque prison of American novelistic formal law that declares: "No efficacious blacks need apply!" A white trustee's panopticon overwhelms and terrifies Ellison's narrative into hiding its best self. Hence, *Invisible Man* is asymptotic with respect to that great circle of actual black life in America where black leadership emerged on the world stage—full force—during the Civil Rights movement. The acclaim bestowed on *Invisible Man* was, at least in part, a function of the novel's cautious reassurance to white folk that fiercely independent black leadership was but an incarcerated/suppressed/cleared/stifled/cartoonish/controlled epiphenomenon of *real white power.*

Certainly, one reading effect of *Invisible Man* is a sense of security for white readers (or, power, in general). This effect stems from the seeming impossibility of black activist intellectuals in America effectively controlling the public sphere. After all, the black woman who kills her master in the novel's prologue is a "dream vision" from the "old days." The protagonist himself is an underground talking head—in "covert preparation" like some Central Intelligence Agency mole—waiting for a better day a-comin'. Full of angst and poignant longings for democracy, his is an autobiographical tale of alienated black intellect in a binary, strenuously policed universe of locked bodily positions: black man/white man, white woman/black man. There is scarcely an intelligent black speaking woman in Ellison's novel—a dutiful wife or a churchgoer saying "amen" is what the fiction normatively musters.

Ellison's protagonist is an end-of-ideology—yea, even an end-of-history—intellectual—out of time, blackly ruminating. He is modeled on brooding voices of Russian fiction and the conservative despair (but not the engaged and sardonic critique) of T. S. Eliot's *The Waste Land.* The voices of protagonist and narrator constitute a veritable archive of white literary modernism. They are literarily "American" to a fault. The narrative's intention is clearly to be the

Great American Novel. Alas! And, wonder of wonders, it worked like a charm, indeed, brilliantly! For the panoramic, completely black-disempowering, white-reassuring view of "race matters" that *Invisible Man* offers is exactly what America always welcomes. Here's Sambo, unself-consciously out on a lambo, working to delight white folks! (It is only after Tod Clifton's death that the protagonist discovers the "invisible string" Clifton used to master white expectations of eternal black entertainment. Can we say Monk's dance was unknown to him, even though he speaks of the "music" of invisibility?)

Tod Clifton is the poster boy for a rainbow coalition of seemingly well-meaning white people. He believes in the radical energies of the Brotherhood. It is when he recognizes that he has been duped by mere self-protective liberalism masquerading as John Brown resolve that he becomes disillusioned and goes AWOL. He is lost in the city, a black man knocked off his certainties by white betrayal. In his disillusionment, he thinks to become a cynical, black peddler of street-corner blackface. He believes, I think, he can distance himself from a slippery past through display of the dancing black puppet-on-a-string that is strictly a matter of tricky manipulations. In short, Tod believes that after such knowledge of white brotherhood betrayal, the only forgiveness possible is deft representation. He is more than half-mad in the city of white power.

We are, of course, meant to see Tod as the "wandering Negro," eternally betrayed by white radicalism in America. His funeral is a masterfully oratorical burial of all black hopes of white help. But there is a sense, I think, in which Tod's death from the "excessive force" of a policeman's bullet is entirely within the frame of a unique set of urban, northern, black realities of life in the white city. White policemen are the death squad for black parody. Tod's attempts to mock the black-man-on-a-string control strategies of white radicalism backfire and result in his death. Though he knows that in the face of a complex and powerful white urban modernity there are always strings (sometimes nooses) attached to black bodies, he doesn't possess the proper black sanity to confront this controlling interest. He is, in fact (in the eyes of Ellison's *Invisible Man*), crazy. In the best eyes of Monk, he thinks there are still audiences to effectively play for.

But there is a strong possibility that Tod goes as far in his street-corner, revelatory resistance as any black man can in America. That is to say, he might actually be right: there is no white help on the way. To get it right and represent the powerlessness of blacks vis-à-vis their own destiny is to invoke both the indifference and the ire of the larger economy. (The response to Hurricane Katrina, of which more later, is a case in point.) Tod is, finally, a black man in the throes of racing thoughts, sad disillusionment, and a bone-chilling capacity for black representational irony. He is akin to Richard Wright's "man who lived underground," and thus, a brilliant danger to himself and to white power. I am not certain, however, that even his creator knew all of this—this correlation between black urban modernity and madness. After all, Ellison's asylum in *Invisible Man* is located decisively in the black South, just down the white-power surveilled road from the black university. Though it be mad, it seems in Ellison not actively to be able to tell the difference between a revolutionary Blackhawk and a third-world handsaw. So, we must now, I fear, speak as eloquently as possible of precisely the South and, yes, mental illness.

The Catch

A Meditation on Family, Mental Illness, and My Father

My reading in sociology enabled me to discern many strange types of Negro characters to identify many modes of Negro behavior; and what moved me above all was the frequency of mental illness, that tragic toll that the urban environment exacted of the black peasant.

—Richard Wright, *Black Boy*

If thou beest he—but O how fallen! How changed
From him who in the happy realms of light
Clothed with transcendent brightness did outshine
Myriads, though bright!

—John Milton, *Paradise Lost*

I was forced to accept what he had to say, realizing even then that if his story was an act of invention then I had to listen as an act of faith.

—Earl Lovelace, *Salt*

What are we to make of the relocation of actual black bodies from
bleak southern agrarianism and domestic labor to a northern promised land? Not to New England's "promise," in at least one instance,
but to the wide prairies of the Midwest, and to cities like Chicago?
How did this movement affect black southern consciousness, which
was in effect born again into a second childhood? Wright describes
the personal psychological effects of his migration from Memphis
to Chicago:

> What could I dream of that had the barest possibility of com-
> ing true? I could think of nothing. And, slowly, it was upon
> exactly that nothingness that my mind began to dwell,
> that constant sense of wanting without having, of being
> hated without reason. A dim notion of what life meant to a
> Negro in America was coming to consciousness in me, not
> in terms of external events, lynchings, Jim Crowism, and
> the endless brutalities, but in terms of crossed-up feeling,
> of psyche pain. I sensed that Negro life was a sprawling land
> of unconscious suffering, and there were but few Negroes
> who knew the meaning of their lives, who could tell their
> story. (*Black Boy*, 314)

That "crossed-up feeling" or "psyche pain," as Wright describes
it, is an interiorization of the ethics of living Jim Crow. It is an after-
effect of the living arrangements that emerged from those transatlantic ruptures of modernity. Wright's Chicago daily life is less an
occasion for physical fear than a black canvas of clinical depression.
(Dare one say, a Fanonian canvas?) However, there is in all this mental anguish a repressed complement of imaginative dreaming. Nothingness, Wright implies, may be soothed by powerful and willful
commitment to an almost unimaginable self-fashioning. Such, of
course, was my father's similar insight. In fact, he and Wright were
born in the same year, and there is so much southernness in my
recall of my father's making his way in an American world that not
even whole sets of encyclopedias can contain it. Yet, of one thing I
am certain and can express succinctly here: my father was a hero of
the high-wire incumbencies of being a black father in an American
world that can drive black men insane and smash them into a wall of

negligence and abandonment with as simple a denial as the promise of dignified labor. We, Houston, Sr.'s sons, all came to understand, as we grew older in black southern wisdom, that our father would never be so crazy or careless as to leave us, no matter what the cost. Our blessing was that Houston, Sr., passed on his resolve to the third and fourth generations of we who love him. Through his persuasive insistence on our grasping literacy and the ability to express ourselves eloquently, he gave us a gift of storying. I, myself—black academic and father, no more or less—have only one story to tell after my foregoing family reflections.

It is a story reflecting my father, his wisdom, his complexities of modernity, his implicit forging of family love and understanding in what is now called the *dirty South*. To my father's mind, the only true sign of family for the black fathers was the salvation of their sons. He knew black men—in southern-shaped economies of race and finance and affect in the New World—must always be resourced to make what he called *the catch*. What follows is a story of mental illness, a father and his son, and the invaluable imperative to action flowing generationally from received southern wisdom.

■■

Let me first confess that I have arrived at the point in life where it seems odd to me when someone defines *family* in exclusively biological terms, as though all one has to do is count the blood relatives and enter their names in the family Bible. I also find it amusing when someone heartily clasps my hand on first meeting and says: "You feel just like *family!*" "No," I want to say. "There's no way you can mean that. It's not right." I believe family is something that cannot be defined easily or invoked casually. After a lot of living, in fact, life has forced me to believe that family is like an orbit in space. It is fluid and always slightly varying motion or process around a single body. That body is the child—your child.

My wife and I met at age eighteen. In the fall excitement of those college beginnings, we became girlfriend and boyfriend. When we married, we became a "couple" (though to our parents, we were

still, always, "the children"). But when our child—a lovely boy—
was born, we finally became a *family.*

The primary state of the family is the condition of the child. His
magnetic and gravitational field determines the sanity of the orbits
we travel. At age twenty-two, our child was happily and safely po-
sitioned. The stars appeared at night, the sun shone by day. All was
right with the world.

Our son completed his course of study at a prestigious Ivy League
university. His plans were to be a filmmaker—the new Spike Lee—or
else a famous scholar of film. By 1994, he had determined he would
write his doctoral dissertation on the gothic genre in relationship to
black horror films. He had made two films at New York University's
Tisch School of the Arts as a production major, and then, having decided filmmaking was for the "rich and well-resourced," he transferred
to the University of Southern California's Annenberg School, where
he held the best graduate fellowship offered. Professor Todd Boyd, the
film scholar and critic, was his friend, advocate, and mentor.

"But wait," you say. "You are rushing things. You haven't even
told us the story of his birth." And, yes, there is always a story surrounding birth, because it is always commencement and expansion
in the universe called *family.* There is a way, in fact, in which we could
say that any story or even *all* stories are ultimately family stories.
Moreover, no loving or conscionable family member would "tell a
story on you" in a public place if he did not have your approval.
Know that Mark has read more than once the prose that follows,
consulted with me, generously given his consent to its airing. Family infuses all through the appearance of the child; it is sustained by
language, and love, and stories. *Crick crack!*

Our son was born on December 18, 1970. He weighed seven
pounds, eight ounces. He was twenty-one-and-a-half inches long.
He lay with perfect stillness—all fingers and toes intact—in my
arms. We had been married and a couple for four years when our
son was born. I was deeply resistant to fathering. I, like my father,
argued against any extension of our relationship that would bring
more American racial responsibility, less spontaneity, and greater
American expense. And I did not, I think, want to be locked any
more tightly into the vows and commitments of what seemed

to be a quite satisfactory marriage. However, once we decided to have a child, my Type A enthusiasm shifted into high gear. I began energetically collecting, digesting, reading, and assembling the lore, catalogs, collectibles, and necessities of child begetting, baby having, infant care, and natal knowledge.

During the months of her pregnancy, my wife and I purchased our first home. It was in Charlottesville, Virginia, situated among dogwoods and oaks that yielded glorious color. In the kitchen of that house, we scrawled chalk across every cabinet, trying out names for the black child who was to be born. What if it was a girl? Would "Lisa" do? If it was a boy, could we name him "Mark Frederick Baker"? I mean, wouldn't the first two initials M. F. doom him forever to taunting by his peers? "So, you think you a BAAAAAD 'M.F.,' don't you?" (Shades of Samuel L. Jackson in *Pulp Fiction*!) Ah, my goodness, the things parents worry about is astounding!

"Frederick" was purely and simply a middle to hold all in place. It was drawn from our mutual admiration for Frederick Douglass, who said, "without struggle is no progression," and "he who would be free must strike the first blow!" Mark was a child of laughter and night terrors who scared the bejesus out of us! As a young boy, he was passionate in his enthusiasm (genetic inheritance, alas) and capable of the craziest surprises. Like the time we had been traveling for twelve hours and, exhausted, we checked into a nice motel. He finished his bath, and we were helping him slip into his pajamas when he suddenly sprang to his feet on the bed and began bouncing up and down, singing: "I want to dance! I want to dance! I want to dance!" What was the sprit saying to him at that moment?

During his senior year of high school, he simply stormed out of our house, disgusted with all that family represents. We didn't know where he was for three weeks. We feared the graduation party guest list of one hundred and fifty might be without a guest of honor. Mark looked splendid and relaxed on the day of the commencement, however, saying: "I love you guys. You knew I was going to be here. What's the problem?" Orbits of the family. Simple adoration. The surprises of family are legion.

We drove cross-country with Mark in the year he decided to transfer to the University of Southern California. At precisely

4:00 A.M. at our Grand Canyon National Park motel, he awoke and shouted: "Let's go, guys! We can't be late for the sunrise." He had decided precisely in what spot he wanted us all to be to watch and film first light, the light that summons echoing sounds of morning birds and brings majestic colors among the rock formations of the canyon. He was both our center of gravity and, in our more earthly imagination, the strong suspension wire of our bridge to the future. We haven't had the heart for some time now to look at the film footage he shot that morning. Daybreak ecstasies. It hurts too much.

::

Mark's first violent, delusional, psychotic crash in the uncontrollable throes of bipolar disorder hit our family in the summer of 1996. In retrospect, we know the horrific, obscene, name-calling, physical-violence-threatening argument at the end of our journey to Los Angeles (on the other side of sublime sunrise, canyon beauty) was symptomatic. At his insistent demands thereafter, we were the fount of a veritable stream of money, checks, loans, cash gifts from the East. The gifts always seemed to miss the mark of their intended purpose. The evaporating money, we later learned, went for alcohol and drugs. We didn't know at the time that their disappearance forecast a horrible storm. When that storm hit with gale-force winds, exploding sunspots, and cosmic eruptions, our lovely boy and loyal son—the one whose spirit wished to dance—was catapulted into an abyss far deeper and darker than the canyon before daybreak.

His thoughts raced him into delusional provinces of extraterrestrial voices, sightings—messianic visions that exhorted him to rescue "the black nation" from slavery, to marshal an army under the flag of Uranus and march among unenlightened whites to victory! Anyone who ignored, rejected, or questioned the validity of his "work" he considered deceived; they were demon forces unaware of his power. His anger was so voluminous, his contempt so withering that his wracked and ever-thinning body could scarcely hold. It was clear when he came into our purview, our earshot, our structures of desperate family attention that malevolent gods of mental illness had flung him down:

> Him [who] the Almighty Power
> Hurled headlong flaming from th'ethereal sky
> With hideous ruin and combustion down
> To bottomless perdition, there to dwell
> In adamantine chains and penal fire,
> Who durst defy th'Omnipotent to arms. (Milton, *Paradise Lost*)

⁘

When Mark reached us by telephone, he was not "Mark Frederick Baker," but someone bearing that name—a disembodied voice strangled by unreliable beliefs, narratives that carried traces of the sulfurous hell of delusion. He was convinced he was under surveillance by creatures only he could see. He snatched a $50 bill from his companion's pocketbook and fled their Los Angeles apartment. He needed help right now. "Mark, where are you? Do you know where you are calling from?" my wife pleaded into the telephone shaking in her hands. She waited, listening to unrecognizable background noise, as he left the telephone in California (somewhere) to find out where actually he was. He didn't know. It turned out he was at a restaurant-and-bar pay phone, in the wilds of Los Angeles County: desert territories never meant for a metropolis.

When my wife handed me the receiver, I asked: "Can you get to Westwood? Can you get to the Starbucks in Westwood? I will get someone you can trust to pick you up there." Oh my God! Starbucks as urban safehouse for the mentally ill?! But to me, then, Westwood seemed an oasis. It was home to my graduate alma mater. It once had a radical reputation for its resistance to the Aryan supremacist powers of downtown and its *Los Angeles Times* moguls. In the moment of madness, Westwood seemed somehow—no matter how illogically—a safe space for Mark to be. (Ah, the desperation of parents guarding family!) "Mark, do you think you can get to Westwood?"

Then he: "I think so. I think I can." And then: "Dad, can you come and get me?"

∷

Any simple, casual, easy definitions of *family* that had been in place before my son's terrible telephone call disappeared. They crumbled with the irreversible onset of bipolar disorder for Mark Frederick Baker—who wanted only to dance, who made a splendid film, who fought to keep his dignity against racing thoughts and, too, made delusions by using drugs and alcohol. He wrote brilliant graduate-school essays on Tupac Shakur and documentary film. He was one of the smartest kids in his class. Then, he wasn't. Our world was unmade. And it was imperative when I hung up the receiver that summer evening long ago to summon to myself my father's wisdom and spirit. I had desperately to think back to what I knew of family futures from my father. If there were to be any chance of resurrection—the restoration of family, of our son—it had to come from a place other than the dark night of the soul into which Mark had been hurled. "Dad, can you come and get me?"

∷

When my father died of leukemia in 1983, his insurance policies were paid; his retirement accounts were full. My mother never had to work or worry about her financial well-being for the two decades she survived him. Born in 1908, and having survived the Great Depression, my dad (as I have already suggested) was a savvy businessman of diversified assets. I could only wonder—as the fear, confusion, uncertainty, and utter horror of our son's bipolar disorder worked themselves into a chaotic drama unmaking our world—what would my father have said about my and my wife's heavy investment in a single family stock—Mark Frederick Baker? I believe, as I write, that he would strongly and kindly have said: "Houston Jr., I only know for certain two things. First, I know the only thing that will be present when you get *there* is what you have sent ahead. I also know you always have to take care of your 'base,' which means being good at the art of *catching*."

The "art of catching"? What was that? Was it like being a "gentleman"? My dad was fond of cryptic, economical injunctions. Without context, his advisements could leave you scratching your head. You had always to understand his advice in the context of his commitment to his family. Even though his early life was lived on stormy seas of parental separation, scant resources, and southern segregation, my father managed to shape a disciplined self and to harvest from various sites of travel a gospel that had at its core the dynamics of holding on to those you love.

It was a remarkable achievement for a man who was let down so often by so many. It is difficult to imagine who first caught my father, given the storminess—public and psychological—of his life. Who first broke his headlong somersaulting? I don't know. But wrists and fingers interlocked at some critical, decisive, and mind-shifting moment of my dad's fall, allowing him to breathe an astonished breath at his salvation.

⁙

The night before I began to write the present meditation, I dreamed I was at an elegant dinner party. There were hundreds of fashionable guests seated at tables with expensive linen. Somehow, I got tangled up, could not stop falling, knocked over a gigantic vase of roses, which washed out over the room. I awoke, splashed water on my face. But when I got back to sleep, I was still dreaming. This time, I was driving a narrow road. I became the car as it flew through guardrails into empty space. My stomach dropped, and I awoke crying.

⁙

I believe the first person to catch my father knew of such dreams as mine. He knew the catch is primal. Always instinctual. When I was ten years old, my father took my older brother and me to the circus. The animals, fire-eaters, jugglers, clowns, and ringmaster were fascinating. But it was the high stuff that held me breathless. And the high wire took distant second to the trapeze. The aerialists ascended

long, chrome ladders to small perches aloft. They set the bar in
motion, gripped and committed, swinging into open air toward the
catch. The Flying Wallendas did it with ease—the daring young men
on the flying trapeze! Would that man suspended only by the crook
and grip of his knees on the other side always make the catch? I remember his naked arms—muscled flesh alone. His face an impassive
smile, until the instant of meeting the fingers, hands, and wrists of
the body tumbling into his catch. An unheard connection, as certain and holy as saving grace. Life and the catch met in interlocking
faith for me that afternoon in Louisville, Kentucky. If that man on
the other side somehow failed the catch, no doubt he would have
unlocked his knees from the bar, hurled himself headlong after that
body tumbling away from him. Life swings just like the trapeze, and
our arms live in naked hope. Family bodies hurtling toward us at
high speed in midair don't allow choice.

The first one to catch my father knew such aerial dynamics as
I have described. I believe this. Because whoever it was, he was in-
stinctually fearless. A teacher, perhaps, who said: "The first failure is
reason. The first and only virtue is love. I catch because I love. Not
to catch is to die, now or later." I add: The late-night depression of
hoarded money and weak apologies is a chorus of death. To catch is
to give birth to possibility. The teacher responds: "First catch, then
hope." My father was a genius at catching. Aptly tutored, he swung
into responsible life instructed. If you do not catch the ones you
love, you die—now or later. My father knew that. No apologies or
forgiveness are available. Hope is stillborn if you miss.

When my father said: "I will always back your falling, honor my
promises, prop you up on every leaning side," he meant it. ("If you
get into trouble while you are over there in Edinburgh, I will back
you up.") He spoke such words with quiet conviction, and fearless
love. His confidence in my belief in him was supreme. He knew
that I would venture the bar *not because I believed in myself* (not, at least,
initially), but because I believed without reservation that *he* always
could and would even to his own death catch me. He was my best
friend before I even knew how to spell the word.

The first and only virtue is love. The only sustainable reality of
love is friendship. Loving your enemy is a myth. Once loved (if,

that is, you catch them), your enemies are transformed utterly—no longer "enemy," but possibility. Their animosity is undone by surprise, and the energy of your arrest.

⠿

As teenagers exuberant in our hot rush to independence, my friend Bobby Coleman and I forgot about the tickets, the requirements, the rules, and rushed past the attendants at the gates of the stadium. We had come with our fathers to witness the all-Negro Central High School play the segregated Catholic powerhouse of Louisville football on a chilly Friday evening. Charging ahead beneath the bleachers toward the stands, we were suddenly collared as if we were crooks in an old Charlie Chaplin film. A huge, red-faced, white policeman had us by the scuffs of our necks. "Where's you boys' tickets?" he demanded. "Our fathers have them," we managed. "You boys is lyin'. You sneaked o'er them walls. You ain't got no tickets. I'm a' take y'all downtown, and lock you up."

At that precise moment of our swing into open air, upsetting the roses, plummeting to the cavernous depth of the ravine, doomed to bread-and-water incarceration, my father's arms appeared—extended, unlocking the policeman's fingers from our shirt collars. "These are my sons, officer." That's all he said. We were beneficiaries of the catch. He was fearless in his love. He was our friend. The policeman was undone. Staring into my (our) father's eyes, he was completely unsettled by the outrageous fearless strangeness of this love. I think he might have wished there had been one of his buddies there to catch him!

⠿

My younger brother once idolized me. I taught him all he knew of photographic darkroom technology, and how to make first contact with girls when he was a preteen. I have not spoken to him now in years. I have an old telephone number that gives me word that the number I have reached is "not a working number." Years ago, I conned him into an unequal contest of wills and bodies. He, of course, lost. My father beat my butt to a fare-thee-well that evening, saying, "This is your brother; you are older. You must always take care of him." I wonder what my father would make of my failure to see the symptoms of my younger brother's disappearance. What would he have said of my failure to catch him before he was gone? It is so easy to get tangled up. The first and only virtue is love. And parents of families dream that if one brother swerves toward open space, the other will snatch the wheel and right the car—because . . . they are supposed to be friends.

::

When I arrived at Los Angeles International Airport on that hot June afternoon in 1996, after our son's so-disturbing telephone call, I carried only a small handbag with a change of clothes, some toiletries, and his return ticket to Philadelphia. However, as soon as I reached the home of the colleague and fellow teacher of literature who had picked him up at Starbucks and took him into her keeping for the evening, I knew things were not right. He looked at me and said: "Dad, it's good to see you, man! It's been a long time, hasn't it?" We had seen Mark just a month before on a visit to Los Angeles. He moved to the sofa in the salvational Valerie Smith's living room, and I followed. I sat down beside him. "Take off your glasses," he said sharply. "Let me see your eyes." I said: "Sure." He stared for several minutes and then said: "You're not my father. Who are you? I'm going to my room." He walked deliberately toward the back of Valerie's house.

Matters went rapidly downhill. A manic, hours-long episode of delusions of identity and loss ensued. Our son was deeply, seemingly hopelessly mentally ill. Bipolar disorder had possessed him utterly. We—Valerie and I—were hostage to his mania. At last, as unobtrusively as I could, I asked Val to call 911.

Given the story of my father's prying loose the hands of a white Louisville policeman from my collar and my trembling body, how awful that I should greenlight her call to Los Angeles police for help. But I did. And there is no going back or changing that history. They came—eight squad cars, white men in black, brandishing guns, telling us to get out of the house. Mark slipped away when he saw them on the porch. I pleaded: "Please don't hurt him. He's very sick. He needs a doctor. Don't hurt him."

They found him crouched—fetal position—in a clothes closet, naked to the waist, barefooted, chaste, and accusing. His eyes said I had betrayed him, failed the catch as they led him handcuffed out Valerie's door, into the blistering air, and into their keeping. Eventually, I followed special police evaluation-team officers—two women who had pronounced Mark as bipolar—to the Neuropsychiatric Institute of UCLA. Mark and I were arriving again in Westwood, but not together, decisively disconnected—in states of solitariness that would have been appalling to my dad.

I saw my son stretched—four-point-restrained—on a gurney in a cold examination room. Was he safe? Would there be medicines to cure him, to rid his mind of his bizarre narratives of unseen surveillance and communication from the outer reaches of space?

❖

"Patients' rights" say that after the Haldol—the brutal, antipsychotic knockout punch of sanity, which was developed in Belgium and initially rejected in U.S. markets because of its side effects and is the first stand of psychiatry against out-of-control mania—and seventy-two hours, a patient has the right to legal redress. If the patient is judged to be "logical" and "not a danger to himself or others," he must be released.

Gothic tales of evil family villains committing their relatives (for ill-gotten gain) to asylums went out the window with patients' rights. But so too did certain family and governmental responsibilities adequately to catch the mentally ill in their falling. After age eighteen, the only way to make the catch, to hold the victim of mental illness for treatment, is to secure his or her consent. Imagine what such a rational choice of consent would look like to a patient in the throes of radical mania or excruciating schizophrenia! The exception, of course, is if in illness the potential patient commits a felony. In such circumstances, the seventy-two hours disappear; the patient may be clapped into jail or confined without counsel in prison to rot. With patients' rights, most hospitals and way stations and staffed medical shelters for the mentally ill were barred and shuttered forever. Large, competent, publicly supported hospitals for the mentally ill in the United States are all but defunct. Those whose brains are broken—if they are not killed first by police firepower—occupy special cell units in public and private U.S. prisons, or make brief Haldol-laced stops at the hospitals that will still open the door to them before they take to the streets once again. Homeless and in frightening conversation with unseen forces—so often today this is the portrait of American mental illness.

∷

Our son Mark was "brilliant"—a misnomer for psychotic cunning—in his mania. He told doctors and staff he was a genius of a graduate student whose whole family was opposed to his independence. He said his work in film was destined to revolutionize the planet. Presto! He was out of the UCLA institute in seventy-two hours flat. He was convinced (and who knows the "truth" of it) that the UCLA institute was a medical experimentation laboratory with blood on the walls—hallucinatory drugs served like cocktails. He felt he had just barely escaped with his life; the wicked schemes to make the doctors say he was ill were concocted by none other than his father. Then our son evaporated—disappeared into air like the many dollars we had dispatched to him in Los Angeles. We had no forwarding address or telephone number. He was simply gone. I had missed the catch in the moment that is the descent of mental illness.

There is so much more to be said of our weary days of wondering where Mark was. He did at first leave tirades of condemnations on our voice mail; then there was SILENCE. Nothing. No one in Los Angeles knew what to tell us. No one—anywhere—deceived us about a cure. Like modernity, bipolar is irreversible. Millions suffer. Suicide claims at least a third or more of those afflicted.

∷

"You cannot go to Los Angeles and search for him because in psychosis, there is no recognition of love, of friendship. Drugs and alcohol and a thousand variations of 'risky behavior' are the menu of bipolar." These were the words of our mainline Philadelphia psychiatrist, who was so necessary and so kind to us. He added: "Take care of yourselves. He may never come back."

It was like we had viewed attentively and pleasurably and were in the middle of an amazingly well-shot and reassuring movie, and then someone shut down all the theater's power, canceling even the emergency exit lights. We were in chaos and darkness. We were alone. Darkness was the reality of all we said to each other.

We had no news of Mark for at least a year. Our psychiatrist had warned us. He treated families who rented apartments, hired private investigators, and bribed their children's friends—trying to catch the fallen victim. My wife and I were believers. No matter what doctors said, or how they advised against undue optimism, we knew we could retrieve the failure of what we believed was our failed catch. After all, in 1981, we had together, as a family, survived the trauma of the robbery of our house by two young black men who crashed in upon us on a Sunday evening, terrorized us, serially raped my wife, and laid hands upon our son, tying him hand and foot, depositing him beneath a heavy spread on a bed. We had lived through all that. We were different. Here, then, was simply another high-wire moment. We did not even consider it a trapeze in the first instance. We could keep our balance, practicing that denial of danger so necessary if you are going to do the high stuff. But we knew, in our hearts, that we had missed him, and were dying inside and out.

⁑

We grew weary in waiting, wrote letters to old addresses, prayed in silence, fantasized a second chance, bought tickets to Los Angeles and put them in dresser drawers, stopped looking too deeply into each other's eyes for the truth. It hurt too much; yes, precisely like that amateur film footage of a Grand Canyon sunrise. It was too much; it was too hard. In desperation, I suggested a weekend getaway to New York. On the Wednesday night of the week we were supposed to take our weekend away, I had a dream of redemption:

My father was alive again; he was driving the narrow road, confidently. There were three of us—my wife, our Mark, and me—in the car. The landscape was familiar. Dad was smiling. We were traveling as a family.

::

After our weekend in New York, during which we saw the brilliant *Bring in 'Da Noise, Bring in 'Da Funk* with its cast of remarkably talented young black men speaking at the end of the virtues of family in their lives, we returned to Philadelphia down-spirited. We could barely move. Then, one Friday afternoon, my wife suggested we go to a movie, and I pronounced: "We can't leave town this weekend though, because Mark is coming home." She just looked at me. We had grown weary waiting, and anything seemed possible when you are weary—the worst or the best. "Fine," she said. "But we are going to the movies."

::

Our doorbell rang at 9:00 a.m. on a humid late-August Saturday in Philadelphia, in 1997. He stood silhouetted by bright sunshine—a waiting, unpaid taxi driver and his car's steaming radiator were at the top of our driveway. Our son was a refugee from perdition, his bulk seared to skin and bones. He could not have weighed more than one hundred and twenty. His eyes were wild. He smelled. He had assorted scars on his face and neck, maybe from shaving or broken pimples. We'd never know. His teeth were putrid. He carried a small, dark handbag in his left hand. (I remembered the salvation kit I had carried to L.A.) He had taken off from Los Angeles the night before, having purchased a ticket with money he had saved from his minimum wage job as a parking lot cashier, carrying in addition to the handbag a framed photograph of a rushing Philadelphia subway train he had taken during his senior year of high school. The lights of that Philadelphia train are blurred as it rushes into the station where Mark is waiting to be picked up. He lost the picture somewhere in O'Hare's labyrinthine concourses around 4:00 a.m.

"Hello, Mark." "Hi, Dad." "How much do you owe the taxi driver?" My wife was all at once by my side, exclaiming: "Mark, Mark . . . how did you get here?!" And as she surveyed him, I could sense her disbelief, despair, reluctance to acknowledge this thing of darkness was our son—returned in disgrace in fortune and men's eyes, trembling with fear and psychosis, awaiting our firm forearms and indubitable catch. "Wouldn't you like to come in and get a shower and something to eat?" I asked. And he: "Mom, aren't you even going to say 'hello'?" "Of course, Mark. Hi. . . . Are you hungry?"

::

And so it began. He was so very ill. Within a half hour, I knocked on the bathroom door from which a conversation was flowing into the hall, punctuated with angry obscenities and clear syllables of changing voices. There were occasional fists to the wall. I knocked harder and called his name. He jerked open the door, wanted to know why I was disturbing his privacy. Didn't I know he had people to talk to? A mission? What was up with me? Our son was deeply psychotic, dangerous to himself and others. Where was our seventy-two-hour hold, our temporary catch?

My wife found a doctor in town on that late-summer weekend willing to prescribe Depakote. When Mark had taken the prescribed dosage and eaten ravenously, the process seemed to calm him. But not for long; his was full-blown mania. Within two hours, he began to talk without pause, even while he was in an old pair of my gym shorts and running shoes, taking, in ninety-five-degree humid summer afternoon heat, endless layups, three-pointers, fifteen-footers in our driveway basketball court. While shooting and dribbling and dodging imaginary defensemen, he talked of his army in L.A., spoke of the man whose head had been sawed open by the CIA to insert a computer chip in his brain. Practically dunking a layup, he spoke sternly of the bondage of black people. It was all so totally frightening, beyond anything I had ever known, and exhausting. The only single thing my wife and I knew was: we got a second chance.

Still, his psychotic anger was relentless, unstoppable, as molten as volcanic lava. There were no narratives of well-meaning, generous, good people who had helped, mentored, or saved him. Instead, his will in the embrace of madness was death on two feet, ready to march into whatever competition with dark world forces he could find.

He and I sat on the deck of our home in Lafayette Hill, Pennsylvania—close to the beautiful paths of the Wissahickon Valley where he and I used to train for 10Ks and cross-country running. I listened to his voice. His tales were incoherent, confessional, frightening. He had indeed been to a place where no one was able to follow or accompany him. I listened as our vintage radio broadcast late-night jazz into the acrid smoke of his endless cigarettes. He would wind down just as the sun was beginning its faint rise. I would say "good night." But, if I checked a half hour or so later, I could see that his lamp was still on, hear him mumbling . . . to someone . . . catch radio jazz faint and indistinct as part of the world in which he was trapped.

::

This is how it began upon our son's return. We hung by our knees and extended family wrists and fingers, strong, firm, and reliant. We sought counsel, psychiatry, books, expert advice. We discovered: There are *no* "good stories" of bipolar. None! The reigning narrative is that the illness is an irreversible horror often resulting in suicide. We were devastated, nearly broken. The ladders became more difficult to climb. The high stuff seemed more like a lonesome valley than a daring adventure. Mental illness was our household guest, our unrecognizable son. Mark remained with us for eight months. We found him a psychiatrist, and a job at a small bookstore near home, to which he walked through winter weather and spring calm, sorting out the world as he went, talking to himself, depressed. Doctors said that if Mark moved away from us now, and went to join his Los Angeles companion in Atlanta, he would surely relapse within six months. The rub? She was not a "companion," but unbeknown until his return to us, his wife, living with her daughter by a previous relationship and our first and lovely grandson. Mark had a family of his own. We now had a grandchild whom we had never seen, who was a year and a half old when first we met him—in an airport in the South! These were worlds we had not known.

::

Since that August morning in 1997 when Mark returned, we have swung over empty, strange, incarcerated, manic, sad, and awful spaces. This performance of caring has left us—in the words of the famous black drama of the 1970s *The River Nile*—"weary . . . but in no ways tired." We have the luck of inherited sinews and the black southern legacy to know that life without the catch is far more horrific in its fortunes than all the imaginable relapses of our son—*or any son or daughter who makes family a reality.*

Mark endures now through punctual attendance at AA meetings, and the side effects of antipsychotic medication, offset by a new marriage to a savvy, adoring, and formidable second wife. He lives with the guilt of ages, the loss of all that ever he once possessed—cameras and poems, subway photographs, film scripts and key chains, friends and lovers. He loves the son we met at Hartsfield International in Atlanta, and loves equally the progeny of his new marriage, equally wonderful gifts of two new and beautiful sons—Pierce Frederick (two years old) and Clark Ethan (four months). They live in the South, walk all over the place, ceaselessly! Our son proclaims his will to live—and his acceptance that the first teacher of my father was unequivocally right, just, and true. Mark insists that his mother and I are his "best friends," and that he must accept, accept, accept—not deny—his illness . . . if he is to catch his sons, to prop them up on every leaning side. He has children, forever, *family.*

◆◆

The famous nineteenth-century poet and physician Dr. Oliver Wendell Holmes suggested in a post–Civil War essay on prosthetics that human "walking" is really our "violent" hurling of ourselves forward as instinctual, erect motion into spaces before us. Evolutionarily, it is what makes us human. What confidence it takes to hurtle forward into nothingness! Only two things make it possible: our certainty that we can catch ourselves, or the certain knowledge that through family we will always, always be caught.

Conclusion
Even God Believes in "No Guarantees"

It is called a trading book. . . . The ledger is but one of more than 400 artifacts, documents, paintings and maps in a forthcoming exhibition on slavery at the New York Historical Society that detail the vital connections between New York and the system of slavery that was an economic engine of the Americas for more than three centuries. "We all grew up with images of 'Gone With the Wind' and we thought slavery was a southern institution, but for 200 years slavery was a dominant force in New York," said Richard Rabinowitz, the show's curator.

—*New York Times*, September 27, 2005

On a Christmas card sent in the year 2000, our son Mark in-scribed this:

HAVE A GREAT ONE!!! (smiles) or . . . frowns—

anyway

you wanna cut it

HAVE A WONDERFUL DAY (it may be your last).

feel me? Even GOD

Believes in "no guarantees."

In the space "to," he boldly typed: **Houston Jr. (?), Jr., My Dad.**

An air of mania emanates from these holiday greetings. Yet Mark's words seem so full of presentiments, hints, and implications that stem directly from the space and place of the American South as I have tried to capture it in the foregoing pages. How different, after all, are "smiles" or "frowns" from "curses and adoration" in detailing the fate of the black South as Jean Toomer and other writers already discussed contextualized it? And the implicit questioning of the "father name"—Jr. (?)—that troubles our son's holiday wishes reflects, of course, complex genealogies of family, relation, kin, and cultural contact well known to William Faulkner, Richard Wright, Etheridge Knight, and others. The ledgers at the conclusion of *The Bear* stand in monumental testimony to black South complexities of "family" in the same way that Wright's inscription of his father's abandonment and peasant sensibility speak to ideas of authentic ancestry and traceable family lines of descent below the Mason-Dixon. And there is on the prison cell wall the black letter print of the only smiling Knight kin—a seven-year-old niece.

The South under conditions of its own ruptures of modernity is always filled with genealogical anxiety and Oedipal angst. Perhaps it is this way due to the master class's institution of the mandate that *all* children in the kingdom of chattel slavery followed the condition of the mother. Faulkner notes the "rutting" of the master class, and its heedless consignment of its own progeny to servitude, and worse. Who—legally and indisputably—is "My Dad"? And what are the awesome offices he must perform in order to claim a just and caring paternity?

W. E. B. Du Bois implies that one of the most profound silences in the space of the South is what he calls the "red stain of bastardy." He means by this the confusion of family matters, the refusal of whites and those lowly European immigrants who aspired to be designated "white" to adhere to the just and humane requisites of even their own bloodlines. In short, the South is a miasma of family reflections coming at black and white and immigrant alike as an insatiable desire for a plausible family record to make sane and proper allegiances possible.

Alas, there is no solid ground of affiliation available in the South as it was flung into existence by that rupture of modernity that was the transatlantic trade. Records of slave life—at least in the guise of "legally attested" rolls—were in the hands of white master writers incapable of fidelity to family and honorable paternity. From the rupture that littered the Atlantic basin with African bones and a history of human cruelty that is virtually unequaled, the South is the *Ur*-American territory of ambivalence. And as such, it is the hybrid, unreliable, uncertain, ever-problematic founding ground of our national life. All American sons, daughters, mothers, and fathers must inescapably—at some point in their national existence—look southward to grasp and assess the often-brutal dynamics of our nation's wealth, racial codes, protocols of inclusion and exclusion, regimens of incarceration, propensities toward "curses and adoration," smiles and frowns.

Indeed, this whole nation seems to be materially, culturally, and spiritually ambivalent territory . . . in so many ways like that southern "green" that rolls from Charlottesville, Virginia, to Oxford, Mississippi, and beyond. Just when we believe we have arrived at a pinnacle of racial progress, dreaming dreams of interracial harmony, a white assassin's bullet tears through the life of a black leader's body. Burning, destructive black rage sweeps the North like wildfire. Convinced that we are the acme of superpowers—untouchable by an Other world—we are traumatized by jumbo jets crashing into our bright towers of prosperity at the tragic cost of thousands of lives. Even while we boast a furiously well-scrubbed and solvent "new black middle class," we imprison black and brown men and women at insupportable rates, under the beastly conditions of a national private prison industrial complex. The smiles and frowns, curses and adoration that characterize our lives as Americans at this historical juncture are those of a nation that has not yet cared, or been able honestly, to address the question of the father's will and inclination: my dad? So many years ago, Frederick Douglass wrote in his first narrative as follows:

> [S]laveholders have ordained, and by law established, that the children of slave women shall in all cases follow the condition of their mothers; and this is done all too obviously to administer to their own lust, and make a gratification of their wicked desires profitable as well as pleasurable . . . [enabling them to sustain] the double relation of master and *father.* (my italics)

So many slaveholders were among those who met in Philadelphia in 1776; the North made so many blatantly racist compromises with southern cousins. The Continental Congress was actually a prenational embarrassment—a racially unethical, brutally incarcerating, exclusionary, and cruel bonding of a lustful, single-gendered "family." It left women, Native Americans, and the black South bound and gagged for centuries. Our nation, one might well say, was founded in the fold and embrace of southern family reflections: the so-called North mirroring bone of the bone, and flesh of the flesh, the South's cavalier derogation of the general populace. These regions—North and South—were bound in their exclusionary drive for profit, privilege, prestige, and power. It was, to be sure, a sour family business concluded in the City of Brotherly Love!

Yet we insist we are past all that. We believe a simple presidential apology for slavery will suffice. We declare that reparations for our family cruelties and complicity are too complicated a matter to manage. Which is all so southern and gothic as to make Faulkner an unlikely Oprah Book Club national favorite during the summer of 2005. We are, as it were, back to the bard of Yoknapatawpha for "national reading" and understanding.

If the South is not precisely rising again, it is certainly a favored global destination for people who want to be at a future scene of our national destiny. Five of the fastest growing counties in America are in the South. Today, global international financial empires once again settle in the South: Prince Henry the Navigator's late offspring; children of Captain Morgan's sugar island trade. The South exists in a "red state" of conservatism, religious fundamentalism, international capitalist incorporation, exploitative immigrant labor relations, and an assumed "regional" white supremacy. In perhaps a too-presentist frame of mind, American national economics today can remind us very much of the "Old South."

There is, however, a generation of scholars in ascendance and a progressive political and activist presence in regions below the Mason-Dixon that seem to promise to make a new family of us all. There is a new southern studies very much in view in the academy; Web blogs such as "Facing South" and interventionist institutions such as Duke University's Center for Documentary Studies and the Vanderbilt University Center for Nashville Studies are dedicated to a new and arguably more accurate set of ledgers and family reflections. If such enterprises are successful, before our life has ended, we shall come to see national and global social justice and economic parity across racial and ethnic lines as distinctively *southern* norms. And we shall behold such arrangements of national life not simply as utopian predictions in the pages of essays and books, but as living realities of life below the Mason-Dixon. Our national green, as it were, our conscience and consciousness, could be redeemed.

How, then, can I—in the promise of such transformation and enhanced national and global understanding—hate the South? I *don't* hate the South.

I don't hate the South. But I absolutely abhor what has happened in the wake of Hurricane Katrina, the worst human engineering disaster in our national life. The complete breakdown of national "emergency response" networks in the face of the disaster and the press conference lip-service protocols that characterized President George W. Bush and his administration's contribution to saving lives in the South were disheartening in the extreme. For many, the bumbling incompetence of Washington and the seemingly dismissive indifference of the federal and the local were far more than infuriating; they were fatal. (The death toll is not yet fully clear. Louisiana alone has topped fifteen hundred fatalities, including in-state and evacuee victims of the storm.) Men, women, and children, poor and black—starving, dehydrated, displaced, homeless—dominated the stream of our national 24/7 news media, despairing as no help came from Washington. In the face of the enormity of suffering and, in part, the *color* of the tens of thousands stranded on rooftops and porches, in attics, and in the New Orleans Superdome, they were labeled "refugees."

One could not help thinking of that earlier epoch in our national history when the federal government included the word "refugees" in the official title of the Federal Bureau of Freedmen, Refugees, and Abandoned Lands. In the face of such suffering one could not fail to think of the Great Migration of blacks from the South at the turn of the nineteenth century. These were men, women, and children fleeing the night terror, Jim Crow brutality, economic exploitation, and other indecencies of a land that lynched thousands of their own while the federal government callously refused even seriously to entertain an antilynching law. Those caught in the camera's gaze in the wake of Katrina are the manifold avatars of American chattel slavery's confinement of poverty and blackness to impoverished, low-lying, unseen zones of our national life—just behind the levees. The median income, we are told, of the thousands who could not leave New Orleans before the waters rose was less than $8,000 a year. One might hold such living conditions and such incomes to be nationally obscene. Even that slippery icon of black affection, President John F. Kennedy, did *nothing* on the civil rights front (maintaining the cautious posture of his predecessor, President Dwight Eisenhower) until it was clear that the fate of the nation was radically contingent upon the success of the Civil Rights movement in the South.

Like our current President Bush, John Fitzgerald Kennedy remained motionless, emotionless, and seemingly uncaring until it was apparent that black folks by the thousands were ready to go completely ballistic and censoriously *public.* One wants to say that once southern African Americans—and the best example was Ray

Nagin, mayor of New Orleans—had dramatically "racialized" the disaster and utterly condemned the denigration of the suffering masses, Washington was willing to fiddle around with end-of-summer, vacationing buzzwords and vain shows while New Orleans flooded. It is scarcely, then, the South—especially the poor and black South—that is to be despised when ruinous natural and human violence deplete, exploit, and destroy the already paltry resources of poor and black folks below the Mason-Dixon. It is, rather, the nation—and, in our present time, a global polity—that is to be called to attention and held justly accountable for the racist indifference and tardiness of response that killed, injured, and deserted thousands. We have had centuries to look southward to see the mirrored faces of our classed and racialized distribution of national resources.

One would like to think that a paradoxical result of Hurricane Katrina will be to awaken the South's poor, white population to the exacting costs of their support of the minions to whom President George Bush entrusts "homeland security" and "emergency response." How will poor, southern whites, many of whom certainly suffered as dramatically as blacks, respond to the portrayal of Katrina's horrors as a "Third World," "refugee" crisis in urban blackface? And how will the nation come to relinquish its too-familiar sense that—like *The Green Mile*—what happens in the South, stays in the South? Certainly, the effects of the worst human engineering disaster in a century will offer and motivate not hatred of the South but a realization that, as Du Bois said many years ago (and as already cited in the foregoing pages): "As the South goes, so goes the nation." Those, of course, who do not take in the historical dimensions of our national indifference to southern poverty and matters of race are destined to relive the worst of our history in the disastrous straits of their own ignorance. Their lives can only be predicted as know-nothing, theme park, anti-intellectual instances of supposedly northern immunity to southern disaster. Such existences ensure there is absolutely no security in our always interconnected and increasingly global homeland. A politically gullible, self-indulgent population is a vulnerable one.

I cannot hate the South, finally, because our son Mark now lives with his wife and our grandsons in Atlanta, Georgia, that Georgia state of beauty and burning children so wondrously evoked by *Cane*. I think of the words *My Dad* and realize the deep, sane stability of my son in this vexed twenty-first-century, post-Katrina moment, and I can without ambivalence proclaim the concluding words of this book: *I don't hate the South*. I want the nation at large to read and understand it. If we do not, there certainly are no guarantees of a bountiful future for our American family.

Suggestions for Further Reading

The following is meant to serve as a reading guide for anyone who wishes to travel with me and with Faulkner in the South. I reference the complete works of Faulkner published by Vintage International. Malcolm Cowley's 1946 *The Portable Faulkner* has been republished multiple times; Penguin Classics' most recent reissue dates from 2003. Natasha Trethewey's collection of poems, *Native Guard* (Houghton Mifflin, 2006), provides a critical, lyrical perspective on the history and legacy of race and slavery in the South. T. S. Eliot's 1923 essay "*Ulysses*, Order, and Myth" is collected in *Selected Prose of T. S. Eliot*, edited by Frank Kermode (Harcourt Brace Jovanovich, 1975). I consulted the Penguin edition of Frederick Douglass's *Narrative of the Life of Frederick Douglass* (1982).

The editions cited of Du Bois's works are as follows: *Dusk of Dawn* (Schocken, 1968), and *The Souls of Black Folk*, in *Three Negro Classics*, edited by John Hope Franklin (Avon, 1965). Arnold Rampersad's analysis of Du Bois can be found in his 1976 *The Art and Imagination of W. E. B. Du Bois* (Harvard University Press; reissued by Schocken, 1990). Rampersad also edited the *Collected Poems of Langston Hughes* (Vintage Classics,

1995), from which I quote Hughes's poem "The South." Quotations from Jean Toomer's *Cane* refer to the Liveright edition (1975). The edition of Richard Wright's *Black Boy* that I used is Perennial Classics (1998). I quote from the 1941 Thunder Mouth Press edition of Wright's *12 Million Black Voices* (other of Wright's works mentioned throughout the book, including *Native Son* and *Uncle Tom's Children*, are available in multiple editions).

Information for the chapter "Libraries of Consciousness" can be found at the following Web sites: Jamie Kalven's *View from the Ground*, in particular his three-part series on the State Street Coverage Initiative, at www.viewfromtheground.com; and the Louisville Public Library's home page at www.lfpl.org. The American Booksellers Foundation for Free Expression and other organizations supported the "Book and Library Community Statement Supporting the Freedom to Read Protection Act," the text of which can be found online (http://news.bookweb.org/freeexpression/1456.html); see also ABFFE's home page (www.abffe.org).

The following texts form the crux of my argument in the chapter "Modernity and the Transatlantic Rupture": Richard S. Dunn's *Sugar and Slaves: The Rise of the Planter Class in the English West Indies, 1624–1713* (University of North Carolina Press, 2000); Peter Wood's entry, "Black Labor—White Rice," in *The Slavery Reader*, edited by Gad Heuman and James Walvin (Routledge, 2003); and Ian Baucom's *Specters of the Atlantic: Finance Capital, Slavery, and the Philosophy of History* (Duke University Press, 2005). The forthcoming *American Literature* special issue on "The Global South" will contain Tara McPherson's essay "On Wal-Mart and Southern Studies." I referenced the Bedford St. Martin's 1995 edition of Olaudah Equiano's *The Interesting Narrative of the Life of Olaudah Equiano*, edited by Robert J. Allison. The quotation from the *New Internationalist* on slavery and civilization comes from the August 2001 essay, "A Brief History of Slavery" (online at www.newint.org). For online information on Wal-Mart, consult Wikipedia's entry on Wal-Mart (http://en.wikipedia.org/wiki/Wal-Mart) and the Wal-Mart corporate home page (www.walmart.com). Brave New Films released Robert Greenwald's documentary, *Wal-Mart: The High Cost of Low Price* in 2005. Extensive information on the life and works of Bob Marley is available at www.bobmarley.com. For analysis and data about current immigration to the U.S., I referenced the American Immigration Law Foundation's *Immigration Policy Focus* 1, no. 2 (September 2002); and Richard D. Vogel's article "Mexican and Central American Labor: The Crux of the Immigration Issue in the U.S.," from *Monthly Review* (June 6, 2006). For demographic growth patterns, see CNN's "Top 10 Fastest Growing States" (December 22, 2005) at www.money.cnn.com/2005/12/22/real_estate/fastest_growing_states.

Sources for the chapter "If you see Robert Penn Warren, ask him: Who *does* speak for the Negro?" are as follows: Robert Penn Warren's *Who Speaks for the Negro?* was first published in 1965 by Random House. Percival Everett published *Erasure* in 2001 (University Press of New England). Orlando Lima published *No Room for Squares* in 2003 (Limachips Press). Etheridge Knight's *Poems from Prison* includes "The Idea of Ancestry" (Broadside, 1968). Harold Bloom's discussion of young poets and old masters can be found in his influential *The Anxiety of Influence: A Theory of Poetry*, first published in 1973 by Oxford University Press. James Baldwin's critiques of Wright, including the essays "Everybody's Protest Novel" and "Many Thousands Gone," are gathered in *Notes of a Native Son* (in 1984, Beacon reissued this 1955 classic). Zora Neale Hurston delineates her tactics of black (in)visibility in *Mules and Men* (Perennial Library, 1990). Valerie Wilmer's "Monk on Monk" was first published in *Downbeat* magazine in 1965 (I accessed it online at the Thelonious Monk Web site, www.howardm.net/tsmonk/db65june.php). Whitney Balliett's obituary of Monk is also available from this site or anthologized in Balliett's *Goodbyes and Other Messages: A Journal of Jazz 1981–1990* (Oxford University Press, 1991).

The edition of Ralph Ellison's *Invisible Man* from which I quoted is Random House (1980). Ellison's essays, including "The World and the Jug," can be found in the 1995 Modern Library's *The Collected Essays of Ralph Ellison*, edited by John F. Callahan. Daryl C. Dance's "You Can't Go Home Again: James Baldwin and the South" was published in the *College Language Association Journal* 18 (September 1974). The University of North Carolina Press published Jerry Gafio Watts's *Heroism and the Black Intellectual: Ralph Ellison, Politics and Afro-American Intellectual Life* (1994).

To retrace my acoustic journey through the South, the following pieces are recommended: Max Roach's *We Insist! The Freedom Now Suite*; George Gershwin's *Porgy and Bess*; *The Best of Thelonious Monk*; Nelly's *Country Grammar* (2000); OutKast's "Player's Ball" (on their 1994 album *Southernplayalisticadillacmuzik*); and the traditional ballad "Stackalee," which has been sung and recorded by too many artists to list.

Acknowledgments

Permission to reprint sections of the author's article "On the Distinction of 'Jr.': My Father" was kindly granted by *Kentucky Humanities*.

Permission to reprint sections of the author's article "On My Acquaintance with Black Studies: A Yale Study" from *Companion to African-American Studies* was kindly granted by Blackwell Publishing.

Permission to reprint parts of the author's article "Traveling with Faulkner: A Tale of Myth, Contemporaneity, and Southern Letters" from *Faulkner and His Contemporaries* was kindly granted by University Press of Mississippi.

Permission to reprint parts of the author's article "Failed Prophet and Falling Stock: Why Ralph Ellison Was Never Avant-Garde" from the *Stanford Humanities Review* 7.1: Movements of the Avant-Garde (1999) was kindly granted by the journal.

"The South," edited by Arnold Rampersad with David Roessel, Assoc., from *The Collected Poems of Langston Hughes by Langston Hughes*, ed. Arnold Rampersad and David Roessel, Associate Editor,